THE SO WHAT

WHAT

STRATEGY

INTRODUCING CLASSIC STORYLINES THAT
ANSWER ONE OF THE MOST UNCOMFORTABLE
QUESTIONS IN BUSINESS

DAVINA STANLEY &
GERARD CASTLES

'I wanted to personally email you to let you know that in my 25+ years of education around the critical topic of mastering successful pitches and presentations, the strategies in your book have already helped me to completely change my approach to a board presentation tomorrow evening and will no doubt do the same for LCW.'

– Jeromine Alpe, CEO, Let's Connect Women, Sydney Australia

'This could be the best investment that you make this year to improve yourself: my former McKinsey colleagues Davina Stanley and Gerard Castles have just published a guide to helping people get traction behind their ideas. It's about ensuring that you've been understood so that you can engage people to get things done. Highly recommended.'

– Robert Lakin, Co-founder, Analytika Research, Tel Aviv

'When I build a new team, these foundations of clear thinking and powerful communication are always among the first practices I introduce. The ideas are seductively simple in concept, but wickedly potent in application. They make anyone in business more effective, regardless of profession or seniority. Stanley and Castles nail it. This is simply the single best guide to the fundamentals of clarity and persuasion in any type of business communication.'

– Houston Spencer, former head of corporate communications for Rio Tinto, London UK

'This book is a wonderful guide for anyone who wants to master top-down, message-driven communication, including an elevator pitch. The book practises what it preaches. It is focused on a few key areas – communicating the "So what?", and it provides enough explanation and examples for you to master it, but not so much that you have to wade through repetitive pages.'

– Teresa Woodland, leadership expert and communication coach, Pittsburgh USA

'I read your book and enjoyed it – good insights and practical applications. It is short enough to have a quick read through the main points and message, and then go back later to focus in on the application. I do a lot of presentations that I have always thought of as Why? [we invest the way we do] and How [we are investing now] (portfolio/market update).

'In the context of storylining I think these could be tightened into The Pitch (which is really *why use my firm*) and Traffic Light for updates (what's going on in the portfolio). The exercise of really thinking about this can only be beneficial so I will try an overhaul for next big event and see.'

– Douglas Isles, Financial Services, Sydney Australia

'By way of background, I have long history in the consulting space and believe that effective communications separates leaders from the pack. And it's something that one can continually work on to improve. Over the years I've read a number of books on communications such as books on writing, storyboards, logic, presentation construction, visual design, and verbal delivery. I've recently read *The So What Strategy*, a book on business communications, and wanted to share my thoughts on the book.

'*The So What Strategy* is an excellent book and provides readers with essential tools for more effective business communications related to writing, storyboards, logic, and presentation construction. Here are three reasons why it will be one of the top books for me to recommend to other consultants and business professionals:

First, the book establishes a solid foundation from a structural point of view. The authors cover fundamentals from understanding one's audience, the drivers for particular communications (for example, context, triggers, and key question), bottom line messaging, and logical storyboards for key patterns that come up in business situations. The book also goes further to suggest concrete steps as to how one might incorporate storyboarding and other elements into both one's own work and the internal processes of an organization.

'Second, the book is differentiated from other books, especially as it relates to addressing classic patterns one encounters in business. One classic book in consulting relative to communications is *The Pyramid Principle* by Barbara Minto (also ex-McKinsey). While Minto does a great job at explaining logical concepts that are pervasive in management consulting approaches such as mutually exclusive, collectively exhaustive (MECE) frameworks and tying these concepts to writing, Stanley and Castles dovetail with the same concepts and also cover seven classical storyline patterns that are suitable for business. These storyline patterns include things such as communicating action plans, suggesting recommendations, pitching ideas, providing updates, and several others.

'Finally, *The So What Strategy* comes in a modern package. While I feel the other two points I mention above are strengths, book's package is one is the biggest selling points for me. First, for the time-pressed professional, the book is a very rich but quick read. I got through the book in about two hours, which is surprising given how rich the book is in terms of content and substance. And yet the book can easily fit into the messenger bag of a road warrior consultant. Second, the book has concrete examples of emails, storyboards, and presentations; this helps readers actually see where communications can be improved and how following the authors' frameworks can help. Third, the book provides concrete tools (such as checklists) and is well-structured for being a quick handbook.

'I highly recommend *The So What Strategy*. Davina Stanley and Gerard Castles have done a remarkable job putting this book together.'

– Steve Shu, Management Consultant, Los Angeles, California (http://steveshu.com)

ACKNOWLEDGEMENTS

In writing this book we are all too aware of the shoulders upon which we stand. We both began our consulting careers as communication specialists at McKinsey & Company.

We learned from some of The Firm's greatest communicators: Sara Roche and Joanne Wyss in the US, Mary Mills in Sydney, and Julie Pierce, Thom Shaw, Ruby Chen and Teresa Woodland in Greater China. Barbara Minto of *The Pyramid Principle* fame was also in the mix, as well as many other colleagues from Europe, Asia and the Americas with whom we shared late-night storylining conversations.

We continue to enjoy the push and pull of working with wonderful colleagues, some of whom trained at The Firm, some of whom bring a different perspective. Our current list of collaborators includes Angela Scaffidi, Louise Geoghegan, Josh Dowse, Jo Wigley, Natalie Hoy and Sally McMicking.

We also thank those family members, friends, clients and colleagues who took the time to read our early drafts and offer us some courageous feedback: Andrew Stanley, Bruce Trewhella, Christiane Gerblinger, Mary Morel, Nick Murray and Wayne Lewis.

Last but not least, we thank our clients, who have opened our eyes as to how storylines can be used in practice, inside and outside consulting environments, in almost all areas of business and government.

Project management and text design by Michael Hanrahan Publishing
Cover design by Peter Reardon

ISBN: 978-0-6484025-6-5

Disclaimer

CONTENTS

INTRODUCTION

'So what?'

At the end of a presentation, business leaders regularly ask one, single question: 'So what?' It's one of the most uncomfortable questions in business.

They ask because they want to know why the ideas in your presentation should matter to them and to the business, and they want to know in one simple statement. You might have spent countless hours, days and weeks preparing, but they want a succinct answer that summarises everything for them in an instant. And you want the earth to open up and swallow you because you don't know how to answer this question succinctly.

'So what?'

If you don't answer this question well, all of your work can be for nothing. Early in our careers, we were both on the receiving end of this question and not ready to answer it. Those memories are some of our most crushing, yet also our most instructive.

What's the solution? To avoid the embarrassment and frustration of not being able to answer that one simple question, you must state the 'So what' clearly and unambiguously at the *beginning* of your communication and then make the case to support it, rather than trying to tie everything together at the end when your audience may have lost focus or interest.

That sounds simple, but there is a secret to doing this well – it's what we call 'storylining'. A business storyline* is a simple map of ideas arranged into a logical order and hierarchy. It can be used to make a complex business case or structure a simple email, for a presentation or a speech, for a meeting or a workshop, and there are different storylines to use in different circumstances.

If you have not worked with storylines before, now is a good time to show you one. The key to a good storyline is the structure, as outlined in this example.

A storyline example

At first glance, when presented visually, storylines look like a lot of boxes with lines connecting them. When populated with someone's ideas in a way that makes sense, however, they come to life.

Here is a real-life example. It's the storyline a team used to map out their thinking about how to convince a Steering Committee that they should push forward and implement a new system.

We worked with the lead manager to pull together the storyline for the Steering Committee briefing, shown opposite. Take a moment to skim it and we will then explain more about how each of the elements of the storyline works together.

This storyline maps the key ideas the manager wanted to communicate. It works through the **context**, **trigger** and **question**, and states an overall idea – the **'So what'** of the whole communication (that BigCo should implement SuperSys). It then lays out the **hierarchy of ideas** that support the 'So what', breaking each of those five supporting reasons down to provide enough detail on each to satisfy the Steering Committee audience. You can see from the diagram that the top-level ideas in this structure form a strong case to implement the SuperSys solution.

---

*   For the sake of simplicity, we'll call all business storylines from now on 'storylines'. We realise this term is used in many different contexts, but it has a specific use here that will be consistent throughout this book.

Example storyline: SuperSys recommendation

Context	SuperSys has been proposed as a replacement for the existing rudimentary Management Information System (MIS) that powers the loyalty program
Trigger	We have completed a discovery process to understand what it can deliver and whether we should proceed
Question	Should we proceed?

BigCo should implement SuperSys as soon as possible to strengthen the loyalty program campaigns

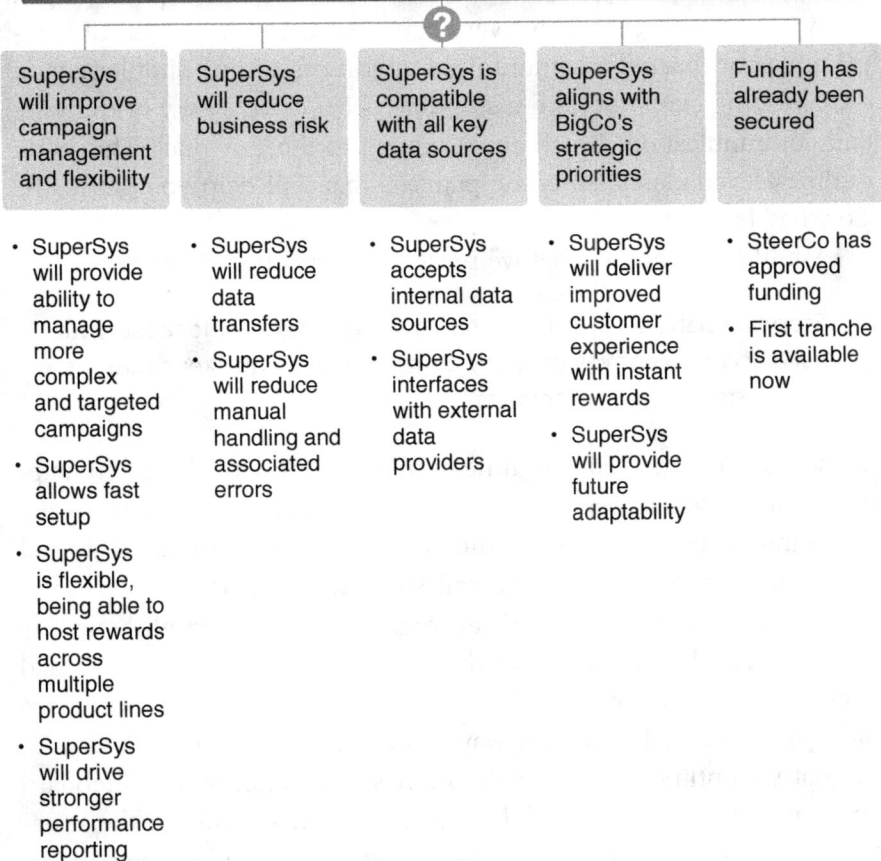

SuperSys will improve campaign management and flexibility	SuperSys will reduce business risk	SuperSys is compatible with all key data sources	SuperSys aligns with BigCo's strategic priorities	Funding has already been secured
• SuperSys will provide ability to manage more complex and targeted campaigns • SuperSys allows fast setup • SuperSys is flexible, being able to host rewards across multiple product lines • SuperSys will drive stronger performance reporting	• SuperSys will reduce data transfers • SuperSys will reduce manual handling and associated errors	• SuperSys accepts internal data sources • SuperSys interfaces with external data providers	• SuperSys will deliver improved customer experience with instant rewards • SuperSys will provide future adaptability	• SteerCo has approved funding • First tranche is available now

> This communication worked. The manager used the storyline to structure a short verbal briefing to present to the Steering Committee. She talked the storyline through from beginning to end, stopping to answer questions when necessary, and she could deal with the tougher queries more easily because she was clear and confident in her recommendation. Surprisingly, she did not need further supporting slides as she was able to answer any question that came her way during the conversation.

This is an example of a storyline in action. It's a fairly simple example. Many of our projects involve very complex ideas. Regardless of complexity, good business communication adheres to one simple maxim – developing clarity around a storyline helps drive clarity of thinking and communication. It's all about getting to the 'So what'. This book outlines seven classic storyline patterns that will help you get to the 'So what' fast.

We like to practise what we preach, so here's our 'So what' …

Storyline patterns are 'the secret' to structuring your ideas so you can succinctly convey your key points, enabling quicker decisions and better business outcomes.

These patterns emerged over time from our work with clients. In helping teams craft business communication, we started to see repeating structural patterns – all slightly different but nevertheless based around common plots, or what we now call 'storyline patterns'.

It was while working with an organisation in Australia one day that we started to think about the power of these patterns. We had been helping the team think through the structure for a complex piece of legal advice and needed a way to cut through the complexity. To do that we outlined some classic business storylines on a whiteboard and asked the team if one of those storylines was useful for the situation they faced. Seeing someone point excitedly to a storyline and say, 'That's it! It's an "options story",' we realised we were onto something, and the search for the great business storyline patterns began.

We've distilled them down to our top seven classics, which are outlined in this book. These are patterns for business communication that help you get stuff done, the stories that help you and your team make good decisions, understand complex issues, monitor activity and respond effectively to problems. These are not narratives in the literary sense, but are still stories all the same.

Once we started to share these patterns with our clients we found that they saved time while also creating more impactful and audience-focused communication. What's more, we saw our clients become confident enough to share those stories even in difficult situations. When clients took a disciplined approach to thinking through what they wanted to achieve from their communication and how they would structure and communicate it, they had more impact and achieved better results.

The seven classic storyline patterns

GROUPING STORYLINES

1   **Action Jackson** – for action plans.
2   **The Pitch** – for pitches and proposals.
3   **Traffic Light** – for updates.

DEDUCTIVE STORYLINES

4   **Close the Gap** – for improvement recommendations.
5   **Houston, We Have a Problem** – for explaining how to solve problems.
6   **To B or Not to B** – for explaining which option is best.
7   **Watch Out** – to counter emerging risks.

Our experience also tells us this approach is cross-cultural and cross-generational. It applies in Australasia, the Americas, Asia and Europe, and it works just as well for experienced professionals, board members and millennials.

Given this experience, we think these storylines are too good not to share. To unlock the power of the 'So What' strategy, you need to take five steps:

1   Understand why mastering storylining is worth the investment (chapter 1).

2   Learn how to use a storyline to identify and harness the 'So what' (chapter 2).

3   Master the seven classic storyline patterns (chapter 3).

4   Use storylines to shape the communication you deliver (chapter 4).

5   Introduce storylining in your business (chapter 5).

In the following chapters we will take you through these steps one by one, and also explain in detail how each storyline works and when to use each one.

We wish you all the best with your business communication.

Davina Stanley and Gerard Castles
June 2017

ONE

UNDERSTANDING WHY MASTERING STORYLINING IS WORTH THE INVESTMENT

You may wonder why you should bother with storylining rather than using other common approaches for preparing communication such as templates, brainstorming or perhaps mind maps. Storylining requires effort because it forces you to think hard when marshalling your ideas into a tight, compelling hierarchy and order that addresses your audience's concerns as well as meeting your objectives. It can seem like extra work when you already have too much to do, but the pay off is immense, and there are huge savings in time and effort in the long run. We've seen it time and time and time again.

Business leaders don't want to trawl through lengthy, poorly-thought-out communication. And communicators don't enjoy answering repetitive and endless questions from audiences who do not grasp the message from the material they are presented with. And no-one, no matter where they are in their career, likes being forced into reworking their papers again and again because they are rejected. This is all a recipe for wasted time and poor decisions.

The problem is that all too often leaders and communicators don't know how to break this cycle. This is where we can help. The first step is to understand how storylining can add value in your business. Mastering storylining and incorporating it into your business will:

- drive clarity of thinking and communication
- drive faster and better decision making at all levels of a business
- build a culture of intelligent collaboration around real business issues
- build credibility and trust.

Let's examine each of these to help you understand why storylining is such a powerful tool.

STORYLINING DRIVES CLARITY OF THINKING AND COMMUNICATION

First and foremost, storylines map the structure of your ideas in a way that is both clear and compelling. Being able to take the complex and make it clear and take the clear and make it compelling is one of the hallmarks of good leaders.[*] You don't have to be a CEO to be thinking about this – you may be a technical leader, a team leader, or perhaps lead part of an organisation. The thinking and communication challenges still exist, and that's where storylines come in.

But how does a storyline help clarify your thinking? In our approach, a storyline is an analytical tool that helps you map your ideas into a diagram in which the ideas are connected according to a set of tightly defined rules. In particular, storylining:

- makes you stop and think before you communicate
- offers a clearly defined set of rules to help you marshal and organise your ideas
- enables you to evaluate the quality of your thinking.

Let's consider each of these.

---

[*] We borrowed 'make the complex clear and the clear compelling' from a speech by a former captain of the Australian rugby team and now business adviser John Eales. He used the phrase when discussing the characteristics of great leaders at a leadership forum for an Australian bank.

Storylining makes you think before you communicate

One of the biggest challenges we face in the corporate world is that people either feel like they don't have time to think, or they don't know where to start. Storylining offers a simple, practical, collaborative tool that enables you to sit back and reflect on what needs to be said *before* you dive in and say it.

Having a 'way' to think through and organise ideas is enormously helpful in laying the foundations for powerful communication of any kind.

Storylining offers a clearly defined set of rules to help you marshal and organise your ideas

In preparing any piece of communication, there are many decisions to make: you must decide if your ideas are fully formed yet, where they belong in the storyline – or whether they belong in the storyline at all.

Storylining rules guide you through this process, starting with clarifying your purpose and audience and driving towards your over-arching question, the 'So what' that answers this question, and the supporting ideas. When we draw it up, it provides a logically ordered map of ideas. At the simplest level, a storyline is shown on the following page.*

We will explain the rules later, but for now it helps to know that the rules are the difference between a storyline and a template or a mind map. They help you shape your ideas into powerful communication that drives towards your objectives.

Storylines look simple, and they can be simple despite the high degree of thinking that goes into mapping them out. The key is to get the right – clear – storyline for your situation, which requires knowing which storyline to use, knowing what the components of a storyline are, and understanding the rules that underpin the relationships between the ideas in that storyline (all of which will be examined later in the book).

---

* Our work builds on some work done at McKinsey in the 1960s, including *The Pyramid Principle: Logic in writing and thinking* by Barbara Minto. The latest and most complete version is available from http://barbaraminto.com.

Storylines have a simple architecture that helps you get to the point

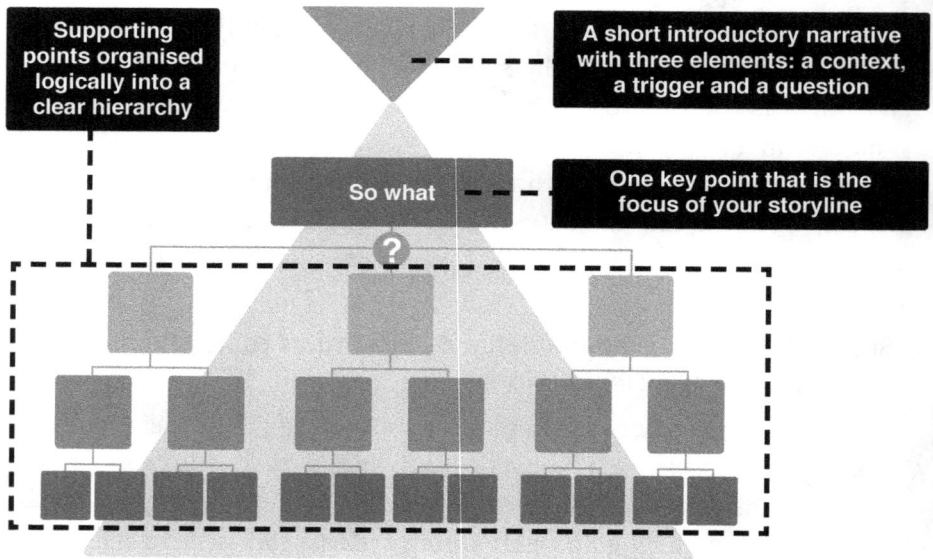

Supporting points organised logically into a clear hierarchy	**A short introductory narrative with three elements: a context, a trigger and a question**
So what	**One key point that is the focus of your storyline**

Storylining enables you to evaluate the quality of your thinking

In providing a clear set of rules to help you marshal your ideas, storylining also provides you with a framework for assessing whether the way you have ordered your ideas makes logical sense, and lays the foundation for powerful communication.

We believe there are four key criteria that a strong, clear storyline must meet:

- First, **the introduction must be right**. It must flow naturally, be relevant and interesting, and zero in on the question you want to address.

- Second, a storyline must **have one clear, overarching idea**. In essence, this states the 'So what?' It doesn't matter whether it's the simplest email or the most complex multi-chapter board paper – every storyline and communication must state the 'So what' clearly and powerfully.

- Third, **the ideas supporting the 'So what' must be ordered logically and in terms of hierarchy**. The ideas should be in an order that makes sense. This is not an intuitive guess but all about logic.

- Finally, **a storyline must meet the needs of the audience**. It's not all about you, the communicator, it's about addressing the needs of your audience.

So, now that you have a high-level picture of what a storyline* looks like, let's see how the act of distilling your ideas into a storyline helps decision making.

STORYLINING DRIVES FASTER AND BETTER DECISION MAKING AT ALL LEVELS OF A BUSINESS

Communication such as the SuperSys example we looked at earlier drives better and often faster decision making. Once leaders understand the issues at hand they can usually make decisions quickly. However, business leaders are routinely presented with material that is difficult to understand, which leads them to ask for more and more information in a search for clarity. This extends the amount of time it takes to make decisions, and can also create significant frustration both within the leadership and in the business.

Storylining provides leaders with the critical information that they want and need. A storyline organises ideas onto a page so that a communicator does three critical things to help the audience make better and quicker decisions. Storylining:

- drives the communicator to form a clear point of view

- enables the audience to choose how they navigate their way through your communication

- increases focus by removing clutter.

Let's have a look at each of these individually.

---

* Our ideas are based on decades helping others communicate clearly and are influenced by the Pyramid Principle, which we learned while working for McKinsey & Company.

Storylining drives the communicator to form a clear point of view

Storylining provides a clear, simple and structured way for you to bring together your ideas, your audience's needs, and the message you need to communicate. It enables you to describe why your data *matters to your audience* rather than just providing a stream of disconnected facts.

Let's have a look at an example using a simple email – like hundreds we've all seen before.

The first email below is a 'stream of consciousness' email in which John just blurts out what he's thinking as the ideas occur to him.

John's 'stream of consciousness' email

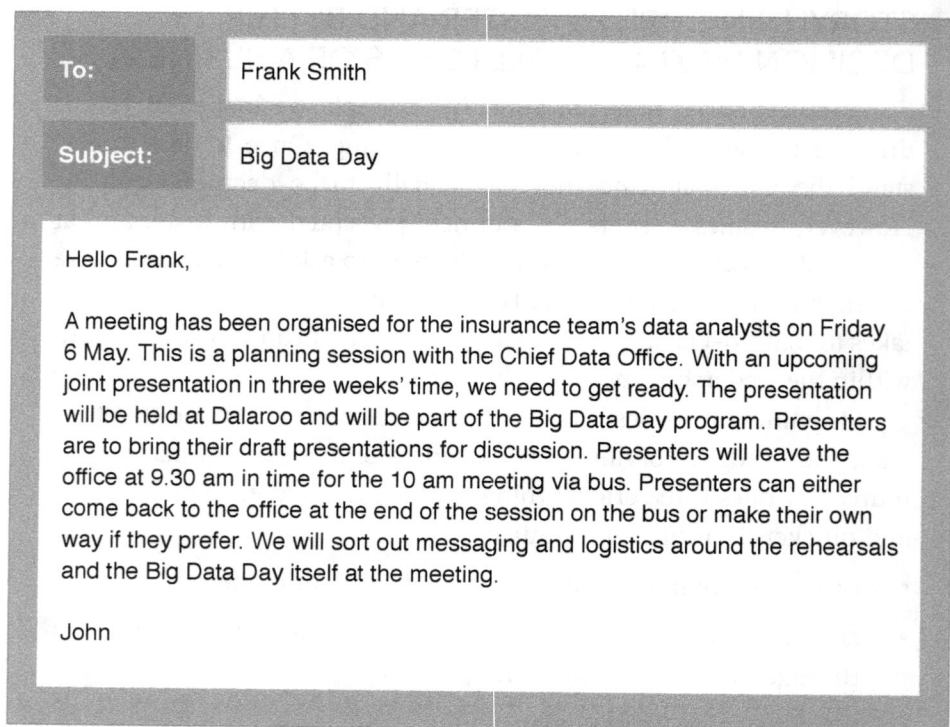

To:	Frank Smith
Subject:	Big Data Day

Hello Frank,

A meeting has been organised for the insurance team's data analysts on Friday 6 May. This is a planning session with the Chief Data Office. With an upcoming joint presentation in three weeks' time, we need to get ready. The presentation will be held at Dalaroo and will be part of the Big Data Day program. Presenters are to bring their draft presentations for discussion. Presenters will leave the office at 9.30 am in time for the 10 am meeting via bus. Presenters can either come back to the office at the end of the session on the bus or make their own way if they prefer. We will sort out messaging and logistics around the rehearsals and the Big Data Day itself at the meeting.

John

The problem with this email is it's all over the place. As a reader you quickly become confused and frustrated, and are unlikely to read past the first sentence or two.

Here's a storyline mapping out what John really wants to say.

John's storyline

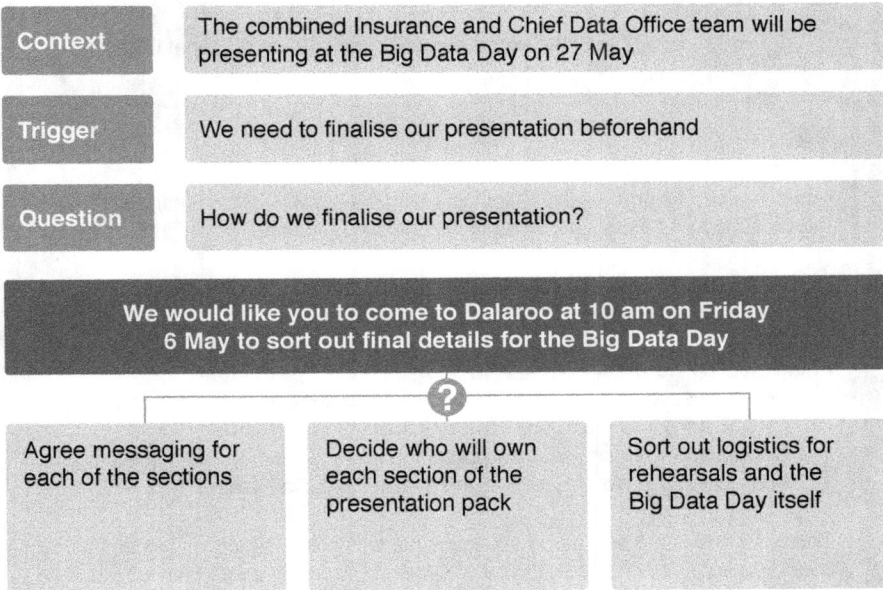

Context	The combined Insurance and Chief Data Office team will be presenting at the Big Data Day on 27 May
Trigger	We need to finalise our presentation beforehand
Question	How do we finalise our presentation?

We would like you to come to Dalaroo at 10 am on Friday 6 May to sort out final details for the Big Data Day

Agree messaging for each of the sections	Decide who will own each section of the presentation pack	Sort out logistics for rehearsals and the Big Data Day itself

Based on this storyline, the next email reworks the same information and communicates much more clearly. It is quick to scan, easy to 'get the gist of', and offers a clear point of view. This is because it's organised to crystallise John's thoughts so that there is one key idea – a point of view – that is supported by a small number of connected ideas.

This email is more powerful

Provides (just) enough context

Focuses on one relevant idea

To: Frank Smith

Subject: Big Data Day Preparation Session: 10 am 6 May at Dalaroo

Hello Frank,

The combined Insurance and Chief Data Office team will be presenting at the Big Data Day on 27 May and need to finalise our presentations beforehand.

We would like you to come to Dalaroo at 10 am on Friday 6 May so we can sort out the final details.

At the meeting we will:
1. Agree messaging for each of the sections that we discussed last time (please bring any drafts you have prepared for discussion)
2. Decide who will 'own' each section of the pack
3. Sort out logistics for rehearsals and the Big Data Day itself

Please let us know if you would like to join us on the bus, which will leave Sydney Olympic Park at 9.30 am, or whether you will make your own way to Dalaroo.

Regards,

John

Organises supporting ideas logically

You don't have to develop a storyline diagram for every email, but each email that is more than a few lines long should be carefully structured. Although this is a simple example, you can see the benefit of presenting a clear point of view, both for the author of the email – who can now articulate a point of view on the issue – and for the reader, who can read and understand the email more quickly and also grasp a more powerful insight from it. Exactly the same process applies for more complex communication such as business cases, leadership briefings and board papers, where the stakes are usually higher.

Storylining enables your audience to choose how they navigate your communication

Too much business communication takes the audience hostage, forcing the unlucky readers, watchers or listeners to begin at the beginning and work their way through to the end, all too often still having to ask 'So what?' Organising a piece of communication using a storyline allows your audience to decide for themselves how to work their way through your communication, and allows them to do so quickly and efficiently. And they'll love you for it.

When communication is based on a storyline, the first section of the communication should offer an executive summary that provides a quick context and 'snapshot' of the story to follow. This allows the audience to know almost immediately what the communication is about and to scan the headlines to find the sections that most interest them. This means that they can choose how to navigate your communication based on their own interests and needs.

They also do not need to read all the material with equal intensity. Business communication is often written for multiple individuals or groups with varying interests, levels of knowledge, and responsibilities. Using a storyline means that each person can be across the topic as a whole and also make their own decisions about how deeply to read each section.

The following Coonawarra Corp example illustrates this. The author of this provides an executive summary at the start, including a short introduction, a clear statement of the 'So what' for the piece, and three high-level supporting points that are then highlighted as headings for the sections of the document that follow. Note that the headings are an idea, a message, and not just the name of a category. This makes it easy to scan and navigate.

We've included the first page of this review here. The full text is provided in appendix A on page 115.

Storylining allows the reader to choose how they read

<table>
<tr>
<td>

The executive summary provides a true snapshot of the whole story

</td>
<td>

Invest $300K to $400K in Black Inc. to build Intelligent Cloud-Based Data Storage

As you will recall from our recent conversations, effective cloud-based data management is increasingly critical to Coonawarra Corp's technology strategy. We have undertaken a review to help us decide how to deliver intelligent cloud-based data storage capabilities – looking at internal and external opportunities.

We recommend that Coonawarra Corp invest $300K to $400K in the Black Inc. solution to ensure Coonawarra has intelligent cloud-based data storage capabilities. Our key findings are outlined below.

- We investigated four options to deliver intelligent cloud-based data storage capabilities.

- Of the four options, we think Black Inc. provides the best solution for our needs.

- As a result, we recommend undertaking a 10-week program to initiate the migration to Black.

Below, I discuss each of the above points in more detail.

</td>
</tr>
<tr>
<td>

The reader can then choose which sections to skim and which to read deeply

</td>
<td>

Four options to deliver intelligent cloud-based data storage capabilities

There are four potential options to deliver intelligent cloud-based data storage capabilities. They are:

1. Outsourcing to Yellow Company: three similar organisations have recently outsourced their data storage needs to Yellow.

2. Outsourcing to Black Inc. who have a well-known cloud solution and who also currently provide three of our major IT systems.

3. Purchasing tools and technology from Pink Corporation: another similar organistion successfully implemented Pink Corporation's technology for data storage.

4. Insourcing to our IT team: our IT team could potentially design and deliver a cloud strategy with sufficient resources and a capability build.

</td>
</tr>
</table>

Storylining increases focus by removing clutter

Business communicators who are unclear about *why* they are communicating often jam in as much as they can on a topic to minimise the risk of leaving out something important. This results in bloated and unfocused communication.

Storylining provides a clear and straightforward way to work out what information is required by the audience – and what is not. Only the information that answers the core question posed by the communication is included. Anything else can be placed in an appendix or left out altogether.

This often results in shorter pieces of communication, and – regardless of the length – always delivers communication that is radically easier to read and comprehend. It also shapes much more focused conversations in any meetings that result from the communication, as the unnecessary and distracting 'guff' has been removed.

What happens after you implement storylining?

Let's hear how using storylines helped these two people:

Head of Tax at a major Australian law firm: 'Previously I would prepare 50-plus pages of advice, but now I can get a much clearer message across to my clients in five or six pages. The advice is the same, it is just much easier for the client to grasp it. The challenge, of course, is that this approach does make something that is very complex look deceptively simple.'

Graduate from a large Australian organisation: 'My boss just told me that today's email was a 10/10. He said that previously he did not bother reading them at all as they were too wordy and too long.'

STORYLINING BUILDS A CULTURE OF INTELLIGENT COLLABORATION AROUND REAL BUSINESS ISSUES

It's tempting to think of good communication as the icing on the cake: the last thing you do to make something look good. However, storylining is an analytical tool that does much more than that. Storylining helps you structure your thinking, work out *what your message actually is*, and provides the most helpful way to engage your audience in that message. In doing so, storylining builds a culture of intelligent collaboration around real business issues, which in turn:

- helps develop strategy
- increases productivity.

Let's have a look at these.

Storylining helps develop strategy

Working with a group of mid-level managers brought this home to us powerfully. We asked workshop participants to divide into groups and build storylines for a piece of communication they were developing in their business. About half an hour in, we heard one group have a 'Eureka!' moment. In mapping their storyline on a whiteboard they had realised they had not been able to get management to buy into a recommendation for the past three months because they had not just been answering the wrong question *in their papers* but they had been trying to *solve the wrong problem.*

The process of working through a storyline together helped them realise that the multiple drafts they had prepared had been more focused on 'filling in a template' than crystallising their point of view about what needed to be done to progress their project and how to persuade leadership about their plan of action. Cumulatively, weeks and weeks of work had been wasted.

As a result, they began to see storylining not just as a communication tool but as a tool that helps them think through a strategy.

We consistently see this in all sorts of work environments. Teams we work with say they rarely, if ever, have the opportunity for intense collaboration around strategic issues. Storylining helps make that happen.

How does storylining help develop strategy?

Let's hear how using storylines has helped these two people:

New global CEO of a boutique technology company: 'In working with a Clarity Coach to think through the storyline that I used to negotiate my promotion from regional to global head, I firmed up my thinking about my strategy for the global business. I also addressed some subtle but important nuances. She pointed out that I was using 'us and we' when talking about my region and the company name when talking about the rest of the world. This subtle shift was critical in demonstrating that I was thinking about the whole company, not just what had previously been my own turf.'

New regional head of the same boutique technology company: 'Preparing the storyline for my first major presentation to the global leadership helped me articulate the high-level strategic shift that had taken place in our business over the past couple of years. Being able to articulate this clearly then validated the direction I was encouraging the leadership to take – and meant I was more persuasive than I would otherwise have been.'

Storylining increases productivity

During our workshops we often describe the convoluted processes we see people using to prepare and socialise pieces of communication – all too often it is a 'chain of pain'.

It goes a bit like this: someone writes a paper and edits it a few times before emailing it off to a colleague for review. That person adds her ten-cents worth (using track changes or a red pen – or not) and then passes it on to someone else, who does likewise. At each step in the chain, people put ideas in and out and modify things to suit their preferred writing style and what they consider important for this communication. This process is repeated multiple times before the paper returns to the author, who then struggles to recognise the paper as his own, but must then at a minimum remove grammatical errors before sending it off for endorsement.

We've seen this happen time and time again across private and public sector organisations, wasting thousands of hours of potentially productive time. A relatively small investment in bringing the team together to develop a storyline breaks the chain of pain.

Here are some examples of successfully breaking this chain.

Breaking the chain of pain

A Project Management Office found that their teams each cut the amount of time taken to prepare their project governance reviews from around fifteen hours each down to around three hours. The key change was for each team to develop a storyline for each review that focused on what they wanted from the Project Governance Committee and the rationale for that, rather than just dumping page after page of project timelines, finances, risks and technical issues into a document. Replicate this across a large organisation and the productivity saving is massive. Importantly, the clarity of the presentations also saw project reviews being cut from two hours-plus per project to fifteen minutes, freeing up the time of high-level executives as well as busy project managers.

A team within the Risk Division of a large bank had recorded an extraordinary 60-plus iterations of a risk paper before a decision was made. That same team applied storylining principles to the next paper they prepared, and after just several iterations of the storyline they received sign-off from the leaders on the first version of the paper.

A mid-level manager from an Australian bank said to us: 'I now know the questions to ask so that I'm clear about what is needed before I prepare my papers. Where previously I would spend a couple of days second-guessing the requirements, I can now have a five- to ten-minute conversation with my boss to clarify the scope and then prepare the paper.'

STORYLINING BUILDS CREDIBILITY AND TRUST

Positive, lasting impact is something we strive for as individuals in business.

To succeed in business you need not only to be visible, but visible for the right reasons – you must have credibility with your senior leadership and your team, and be trusted. You need to be seen as someone who has a strong grasp of the technical aspects of your area. But being technically good is not enough. Real impact is more than 'output', it's the ability to persuade. A former McKinsey Director* captured it in this formula:

Input × Smarts = Output

Output × Persuasive ability = Impact

---

*   This formula was coined by Clem Doherty, a partner in McKinsey's Australian office, and it spread widely.

To persuade, you must have a clear point of view, and also the ability to engage your team, stakeholders and your leaders in that point of view. If you can deliver that you have real impact.

We believe that being able to pull information into a tight storyline is central to persuasive ability and therefore impact. This is because storylining:

- ensures you engage your audience quickly
- builds confidence
- enables you to answer the tough questions.

Let's dig into each of these more deeply.

Storylining ensures you engage your audience quickly

Storylining requires you to identify the core question you want your audience to ask, and then to answer that question in a single sentence. It's about having and expressing a clear point of view: the 'So what'. When you develop a storyline, the 'So what' is not buried. It's the focus of the communication and stated up front. Do that and you engage your audience – fast.

It's obvious, but you have to know the question to be able to provide the answer. We believe identifying the single high-level question you want your audience to ask requires you to take a view on your audience and get to the heart of what they want from you, and then to balance that with what you want to communicate. And answering that question in just one sentence leaves no room for waffle, and builds your credibility. You will have no choice but to be succinct. Your position will then be explained, or perhaps defended, in your supporting points, which is exactly what senior people in business want you to do. They want you to be bold and to have an opinion that you can back up. They can then have a healthy debate with you and decide if they agree or not. This is often the difference between people who are technical experts and people who are leaders who have credibility and the trust of those around them.

Storylining builds confidence

Confidence is everything. We see people we work with grow in confidence and stature within their teams and organisations when they can communicate a clear, well-thought-through and persuasive storyline. Some become well-known for it and build their careers around it.

Storylining is the perfect tool for helping you draw insights from all the details, so you can show your audience what the forest looks like (not just the trees). Thinking through the storyline in advance allows you to set the agenda and lead the discussion, whether it's a stand-up project meeting or high-powered board presentation. Once you as the communicator are confident about this you can engage your audience in both the high-level insights and the relevant details, and communicate confidently even about unfamiliar topics.

Storylining enables you to answer the tough questions

When preparing a storyline you are by necessity thinking through every idea you need to communicate and organising each into a hierarchy that supports one single idea. This is your main point – your 'So what'.

In systematically building a storyline, being confident that each idea is in its logical place and that all necessary ideas are covered, you are ready to answer any question your audience has for you because you know your material intimately. And you also know where the questions are likely to arise. As one client put it after using our approach to prepare a challenging proposal for a $1 million piece of consulting work: 'It meant that I was not "talking bubbles". I had thought through every point we needed to make and could answer any question they had for us.'

* * * * *

The key takeaway we hope you will derive from these examples is that storylining is much more than just a writing technique. It's about getting the thinking right that leads to clear communication, as well as offering a host of other benefits for your business and your own career success.

The next step for you is to familiarise yourself with how storylines work in chapter 2, before we introduce the classic patterns we believe you need to master in chapter 3.

TWO

LEARNING HOW TO USE STORYLINES TO IDENTIFY AND HARNESS THE 'SO WHAT'

Okay, now it's time to get technical.

As Picasso said, we should 'learn the rules like a pro so we can break them like an artist'. We can only use rules if we know what they are, and we can only consistently use them to powerful effect if we master them.

This also applies to storylines. To get the most out of storylines we need to think of them as an analytical tool held together by a set of rules. Without the rules, a storyline becomes just another template with places to dump ideas, rather than a tool that helps us work out what those ideas are and how to put them together to form a clear, compelling piece of communication.

We have laid the rules out here as simply as possible, and encourage you to become familiar with them before diving into the storyline patterns.

We believe there are three key things you need to know before you can unlock the power of the seven classic storylines that we'll introduce in the next chapter:

- what to think about *before* building your storyline
- how to structure a storyline
- how to test if a storyline is fit for purpose.

Let's work through these one by one.

WHAT TO THINK ABOUT *BEFORE* BUILDING YOUR STORYLINE

As soon as we have a communication task ahead of us, most of us are immediately tempted to start building charts, preparing a presentation pack or writing. Producing these things makes us feel like we're making progress.

Taking time to think can be harder to justify to ourselves. At the very first point of preparing a storyline, however, we encourage you to do just that, and in particular to think about three things: your purpose, your audience, and the communication medium that will best meet your objectives.

Great business communicators think these through carefully using a structured approach. This is because they are interested in both creating powerful communication and being time efficient.

We use a three-step framework to help communicators prepare and share a piece of communication – our Design, Develop, Deliver framework, shown on the following page. In this chapter we will look at steps 1 and 2 (design and develop), and then after explaining the storyline patterns to you in chapter 3, we will explain how to deliver your communication in chapter 4.

Design, Develop, Deliver framework

Deliver communication
- Package it (email, prose, pack, etc.)
- Communicate it (clearly, powerfully)
- Get feedback (so you can continuously improve)

Design strategy
- Purpose: I want my audience to …
- Audience: decision makers, influencers, others …
- Medium: pack, paper, email, verbal, meeting, other?
- Process: sign offs, delivery deadlines

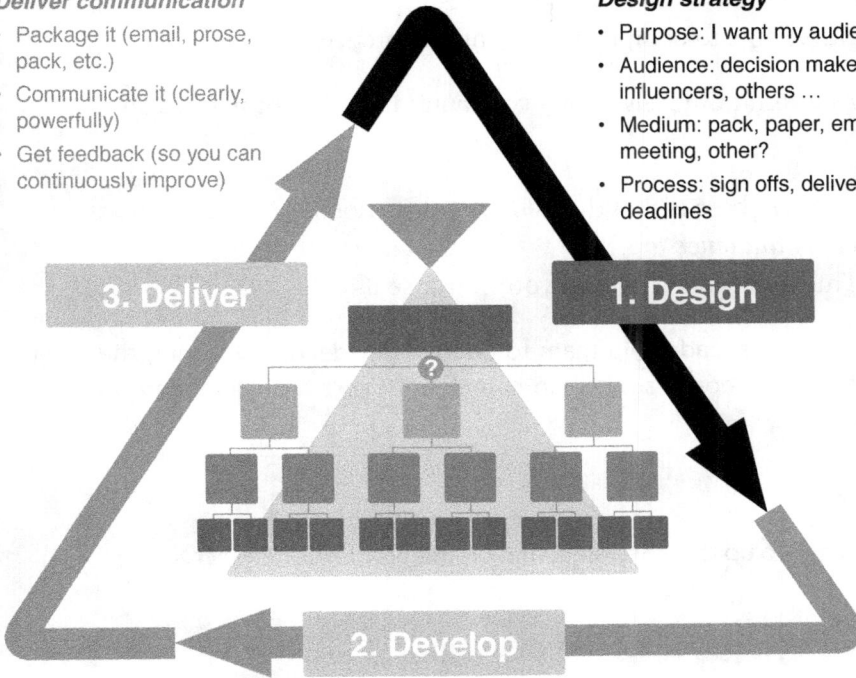

3. Deliver

1. Design

2. Develop

Develop storyline (with a pattern or without)
- Clarify introduction (context, trigger, question)
- Articulate 'So what' (powerful, less than 25 words)
- Map out logical support (grouping or deductive)
- Test the storyline (with 10-Point Test, peers and stakeholders)

So let's now consider the 'Design' phase, which involves:

- clarifying your purpose
- understanding your audience deeply
- deciding the best medium for delivering your communication
- keeping across the process.

Let's work through these one by one.

Clarifying your purpose

Clarifying your purpose is all about clarifying what you want your audience to know, think or do as a result of your communication. You should be able to complete one simple sentence:

> **As a result of receiving my communication, I want my audience to …**

The subtlety here is that this sentence does not say *I want to* but rather *I want my* **audience** *to …*

This leads you to phrase your purpose like this:

> **I want the leadership team to endorse my decision to bring the project in house so we can complete Project X on time and on budget.**

And not …

> **I want to update the leadership on the progress of Project X.**

Understanding your audience deeply

Deeply understanding your audience involves thinking about who they are (really), what they care about, and what style will best engage them. Let's have a look:

- **Who they are:** You need to first identify who the decision maker/s are, who will influence the decision, and who else needs to be considered, as often you will deal with multiple audiences. If you are informing or explaining, rather than asking for a decision to be made, it's still worth thinking through who is responsible for the area you are discussing and who else should be considered, to ensure you achieve your objective.

- **What they care about:** The simplest question to ask yourself here is: 'What is keeping each of my audience members "up at night" about my topic?' And then ask yourself whether the interests of the audience members are relatively similar or significantly different.

If significantly different, you need to make some decisions before you proceed:

- Will one piece of communication be sufficient to meet my objective, given the audience interests are quite different?

- If one is enough (or the only option available), should you spend time with some or all the audience members to thrash through their issues?

- If one is not enough, go back to the beginning and revise your strategy to include a new purpose for each audience to lay the foundation for separate stories for them.

- **What style will best engage this audience:** We find that digging deeper into our audience's working styles helps us understand our audience's needs, even when we need to communicate to large groups. You need to think through whether your audience wants detail or just a quick overview, and what type of information they need.

  The framework we use to do this is the Work Styles framework, developed by Richard and Dorothy Bolton, often called the 'Bolton and Bolton' framework. It's a simple framework derived from the Myers–Briggs Type Indicator (MBTI), which focuses on people's behaviours at a particular point in time and in a particular place. We are, after all, the same people wherever we are, but we behave differently at home compared to when we are at work. We also grow and mature and change our behaviour over time. We won't go into detail here, but we encourage you to get a copy of *People Styles at Work: Making bad relationships good and good relationships better* – details are in the bibliography.

Deciding the best medium for delivering your communication

You also need to think about the medium you will use to communicate your storyline. It might be a presentation pack, a detailed report, a memo, or a one-page discussion guide to support face-to-face meetings with a high-level executive. We're largely agnostic about the medium. The mode of delivery though will shape the storyline to some extent, both in terms of the level of support needed and the type of storyline you use.

If, for example, you have a five-minute quick update, you don't need a lot of detail. On a major report, however, you may have to use several levels of support to make sure your storyline is watertight.

The communication medium may also shape the structure of your storyline. If, for example, you're working on a major government report with an expectation that it might be 100-plus pages long with additional appendices, it may be better to structure it as a grouping of separate recommendations rather than a single deductive storyline. A grouping would be easier for the reader to absorb, rather than a deductive storyline where the reader must absorb the major and minor premise sections before reaching the final 'therefore' section. (Grouping and deductive storylines are discussed in detail later in this chapter.)

Keeping across the process

This section doesn't warrant much detail, but it's worth highlighting the importance of being on top of the process you will need to go through to prepare your communication. For example, are you sure you know who you need to get sign-offs from? Are they around when you need them? Do you need to work to their schedules? What are the overarching deadlines for papers such as yours? Are they driven by a meeting cycle for a leadership team, for example? Knowing the details of the approval process will enable you to set your own deadlines and focus your own work when preparing your communication.

The next step will take your thinking to a whole new level when you create your storyline.

HOW TO STRUCTURE A STORYLINE

Once you have made decisions on your purpose, audience, medium and process, you will want to structure your storyline. You can do this either by beginning with a loose set of ideas and working through the process step by step to organise them into a storyline, or using a pattern as a guide. Either way, you need to understand how the story-lining rules work.

This brings us to step 2 in our Design, Develop, Deliver framework.

Design, Develop, Deliver framework

Deliver communication
- Package it (email, prose, pack, etc.)
- Communicate it (clearly, powerfully)
- Get feedback (so you can continuously improve)

Design strategy
- Purpose: I want my audience to …
- Audience: decision makers, influencers, others …
- Medium: pack, paper, email, verbal, meeting, other?
- Process: sign offs, delivery deadlines

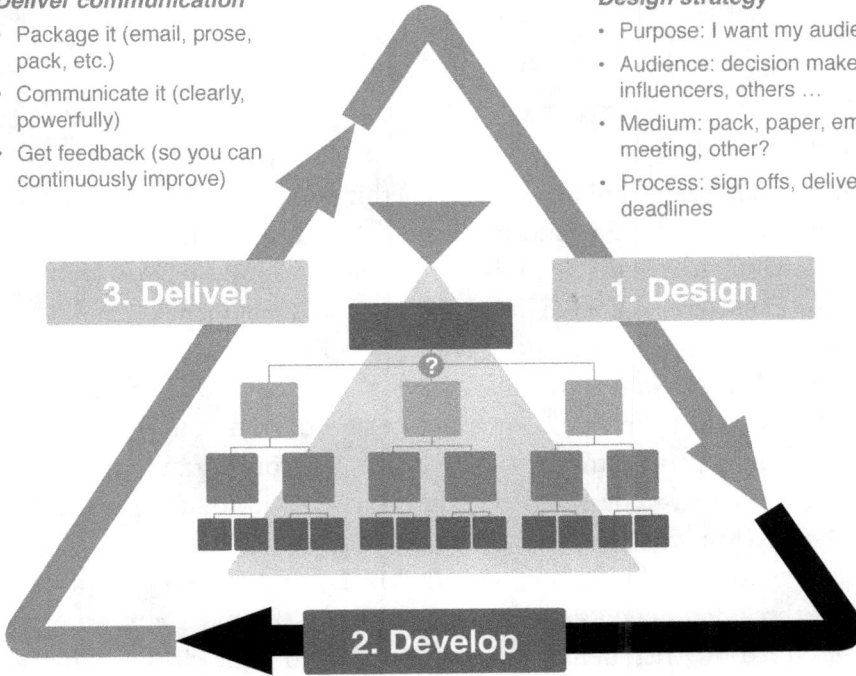

3. Deliver

1. Design

2. Develop

Develop storyline (with a pattern or without)
- Clarify introduction (context, trigger, question)
- Articulate 'So what' (powerful, less than 25 words)
- Map out logical support (grouping or deductive)
- Test the storyline (with 10-Point Test, peers and stakeholders)

There are three basic components of a business storyline, each of which has a central role to play in both clarifying the author's thinking and presenting the ideas to the audience. These are:

- the **introduction**, which helps your audience quickly see where you are headed (this is represented by the upside-down triangle at the top of the storyline)

- the **'So what'** – think of this as the 'big idea' for the whole communication (this is the idea at the heart of the storyline)

- the **ideas that support** the 'So what' and provide as much detail as necessary (these are the supporting ideas mapped out below the 'So what').

Let's discuss each of these in turn.

The introduction

When we have been thinking about something for a while it's easy to dive quickly into the detail and forget that our audience has not been doing likewise. To avoid this problem, storylines always begin with a short introduction designed to help both you and the audience. A good introduction will pique your audience's interest in your topic and draw them towards your main point – the 'So what'. Crafting it will also force you to focus more closely on your audience's needs over your own.

Preparing a good introduction can take a surprising amount of effort. You need to understand the key to a good introduction, and know how to test whether you have applied this well.

The key to a good introduction is that it should form a mini story that has three components – components that as far we know were first described by Aristotle in *Poetics*.* He identified three classic components of a narrative: a situation, a complication, and a resolution. (In our structure the resolution is the 'So what'.) You can use the same approach to lead your audiences towards your 'So what':

- The **context**, which Aristotle called a 'situation', is the commonly agreed starting point for you and your audience for *this piece* of communication.

- The **trigger**, which Aristotle called a 'complication', describes what has changed that is leading you to communicate to your audience *right now*.

- The **question** is the single most important question *you want your audience to ask you* about your topic, which will naturally flow from the context and trigger. Picture your audience and imagine

---

* Aristotle discussed the elements of narrative flows in *Poetics*. Barbara Minto referenced this language in her work *The Pyramid Principle*. We have modernised the language to reduce confusion about the purpose of the second element in business communication (the trigger, or complication). The trigger describes what changed that has led you to communicate with your audience. Simply put, it's the reason for communicating. It's not necessarily a negative factor – it could be an opportunity.

them asking you the question that naturally occurs to them after you have introduced the context and trigger. If you are unclear about the question they will ask you, you will be even less clear about the answer!

We call this the **CTQ**. Let's see how this works. Here's an example of an introduction that *does not* work well:

- **Context:** SurfCo is Sydney's oldest surfboard manufacturer, historically manufacturing 45% of surfboards available globally.

- **Trigger:** However, our market share is falling, and last financial year we manufactured only 40% of boards sold globally. Our research suggests that consumers are now asking for more features.

- **Question:** How can we regain our market share?

In this example there is a flow from the **context** to the **trigger**, but the second sentence in the trigger comes out of nowhere and does not lead directly to the **question**. The flow is not tight enough to lead the audience to the *one question you want them to ask*.

Here's an example of an introduction for this same situation that does lead to the *one question you want them to ask*:

- **Context:** Last financial year SurfCo saw increased competition cut our share of global surfboard sales from 45% to 40%, which we want to regain.

- **Trigger:** Our research suggests that the fall in both sales and market share stems from competition from new manufacturers aggressively promoting innovatively designed boards.

- **Question:** How can we compete with these new players to regain our market share?

Can you see the difference between the two examples? The second is a much more effective introduction as the **context** states the topic, and the **trigger** provides the reason for the discussion, and naturally leads the audience to ask how SurfCo can compete with these new players to regain market share. This is the one **question** you want your audience to ask.

Here are the rules that will help you craft your introductions.

Six rules for introductions

The introduction must set the right scene:

1 Contain a context, trigger and question.
2 Contain information that either is, or should be, known to the audience.
3 Lead to the central question you want your audience to ask.

Context
Trigger
Question

Each element must do its 'job':

1 The context starts the story at the right place in time.
2 The trigger describes why we are communicating with this audience now.
3 The question is the one high-order question we want our audience to ask so we can answer it.

Clarifying this part of your story can be tough, but making certain that just one **question** will flow naturally from the **context** and **trigger** will lead you to the right question and increase your chances of getting to a 'So what' that deals with the issue at hand. We find it often pays to develop a draft CTQ, and then revisit it and finalise it once you have sketched out the storyline.

The 'So what' (the 'big idea' for the whole communication)

Now that you have clarified the question you want your audience to ask and you know how you will lead them to it with a great introduction (the CTQ), you need to answer it in one short, clear and powerful sentence. This sentence forms the glue that holds your storyline together, synthesises all the ideas grouped below, and must be supported logically. This is the 'So what' that so many business audiences yearn for, and yet are denied due to poor communication. A good 'So what' is insightful, succinct, and addresses the issue at hand.

Continuing our SurfCo example, here is a *poor* example of a 'So what':

Offer $500,000 for a share of the Swell Boards start-up.

This 'So what' is not complete, nor is it sufficiently powerful to engage most business audiences in the need to invest in a new business idea, which means that it fails one of the critical tests for the 'So what'. The 'So what' must:

1. answer your audience's question (precisely: the connection must be tight)

2. unify your whole story (forcing you to cull disconnected ideas)

3. be one idea, framed as one succinct sentence (no cheating – check it really is just one idea)

4. synthesise or summarise the supporting ideas (which we will look at next); it's not enough to be one idea – it must also synthesise or summarise the entire storyline

5. be powerful and supportable (it's not enough to have a single sentence if it is not impactful: it must add value).

Five rules for the 'So what'

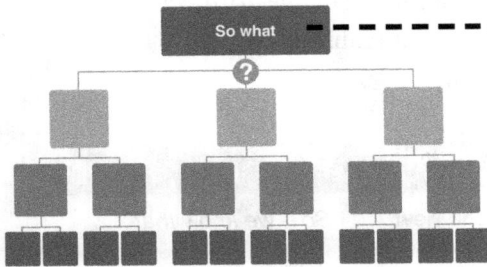

The governing idea must:

1. Answer your audience's question.

2. Unify the whole story.

3. Be one idea, framed as one succinct sentence (25 words or less).

4. Synthesise or summarise the supporting ideas.

5. Be powerful and supportable.

Here's an example of a powerful 'So what':

SurfCo should offer $500,000 for 51% of the Swell Boards start-up to regain market share from competitors within the next two years.

Following is another set of five 'So what' examples. Before you read them, please note one important thing. The 'So what' for a storyline will work best within its context, and we are providing these without any context at all. Even though we say here that the first three examples are not strong from a technical standpoint, they may suit a particular context. For this example, let's say SurfCo management want to know what they should do to pass a looming factory safety audit.

So, to dig in. This example takes a potential scenario from the SurfCo context and illustrates the progression in someone's thinking from loose to tight, soft to powerful, as they clarify what their 'So what' should say.

As you work down the list you can see the thinking clarifies and the message gets stronger. The first three would lead the author to be confronted with that awful question, 'So what?', because the ideas are obvious, not insightful. Of course they should be concerned about meeting the new standards, and of course they should take steps to meet the new standards. It is most unlikely that it would be relevant to explain that it's possible to change their manufacturing processes to meet the new safety standards, as it would imply that their existing processes are so sub-par that it's a major challenge to meet the new standards or that the new standards are unrealistic.

Scan them and see what you think.

Potential 'So what' statements	Evaluation
SurfCo is concerned about meeting the new manufacturing safety standards	*So – we know that ...*
SurfCo should take steps to meet the new manufacturing safety standards	*What type of steps?*
SurfCo can change their manufacturing processes to meet the new manufacturing safety standards	*Change in what way?*
SurfCo should devote extra resources now to reorganise their manufacturing processes to meet the new safety standards	*Okay – clear, powerful*
SurfCo should devote extra resources now to address potential safety breaches so it qualifies with the new manufacturing safety standards before the February 28 deadline	*Strong – clear, powerful and specific*

So, that's how to create a good 'So what', and it is the lynchpin of a good storyline. It's what you are working towards with your whole communication.

Let's now look at how to organise your ideas to support the 'So what'.

The supporting ideas

The ideas supporting the 'So what' must be arranged so they make sense to the audience. To do this, you must revisit who they are, what they know about the topic in question, and what they might want to know about it.

Let's continue with our example …

When deciding how to structure the ideas to communicate to the audience – the leadership at SurfCo – the team would think about the leadership's needs *before* choosing a structure. They would approach the communication differently if leadership *already knew* about the Swell Boards start-up and were across the alternatives, compared to if *they did not know* much about the start-up or the option to buy into the business.

There are two ways to logically present the supporting ideas in a storyline:

- using a **grouping structure**
- using a **deductive structure**.

Let's consider each of these and how they could work in the SurfCo example, depending on what the leadership team already knew about the available options.

*The grouping structure (enables you to explain why, how **or** what)*
A **grouping structure** enables you to address *why* something is so, *how* it should be implemented, or more simply '*what* it is'.

At the simplest level, a logical grouping structure looks like the diagram on the following page.

Logical grouping

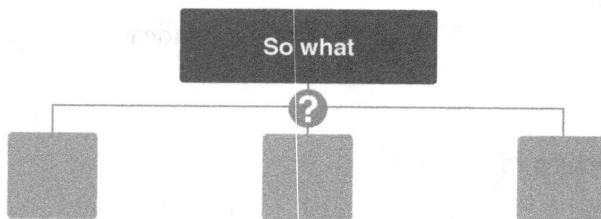

It's a structure in which a small number of separate ideas (the lighter grey boxes) grouped together are sufficient to support and answer the question raised by the 'So what'.

The SurfCo team might use a structure like this for SurfCo's leadership if they were confident that leadership wanted to know either *why* to choose to invest in Swell Boards or *what steps to take* to purchase 51% of Swell Boards. At the top level of the grouping structure there is room to discuss either why or how, but not both.

Let's assume that SurfCo's leadership wants to know *why* Swell Boards might be a good investment, and the discussion on *what steps to take* might come later. If this were the case, on the following page is a potential grouping structure that the team could use to discuss their recommended investment with the leadership team.

For a storyline about a significant investment such as this, the team would most likely use the storyline as the outline for a presentation pack or a prose-style paper. This allows them to present the high-level ideas and provide supporting evidence for each of the key points.

For now, though, our focus is on getting the thinking right. We'll talk more about how to present storylines later.

Grouping storyline: SurfCo example

Context
Last financial year SurfCo saw increased competition cut our share of global surfboard sales from 45% to 40%.

Trigger
Our research suggests that the fall in both sales and market share stems from competition from new manufacturers aggressively promoting innovatively designed boards.

Question
How can we compete with these new players to regain our market share?

SurfCo should offer $500,000 for 51% of Swell Boards to stave off competitors which are investing in ways to make surfboards more 'forgiving'

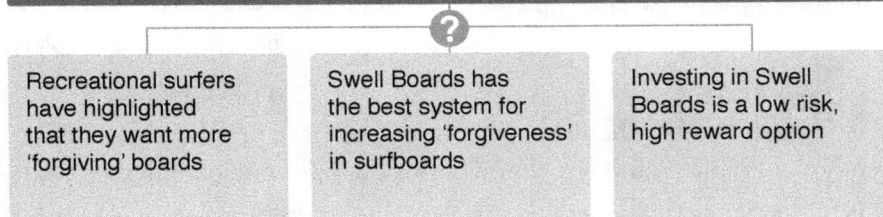

| Recreational surfers have highlighted that they want more 'forgiving' boards | Swell Boards has the best system for increasing 'forgiveness' in surfboards | Investing in Swell Boards is a low risk, high reward option |

- 38% of the surfers we interviewed indicated that they wanted a board that was more 'forgiving', which they defined as stable and easy to use, given they are not pro surfers

- 10% of recreational surfers indicated that they have considered giving up surfing because it is too hard to master

- No other single idea that might improve surfboards appealed to more than 5% of the recreational surfers we interviewed

- Swell Boards has the most advanced and effective system with patents approved

- SurFree has a clever system that we give only a 5/10 for effectiveness

- Three other start-ups are experimenting with ideas, but none have yet progressed to a serious round of testing

- Swell Boards is at a point in their growth where cashflow is limiting their ability to deliver on fast growing numbers of orders quickly enough

- Swell Boards sees us as their preferred investor

- $500,000 is a small investment for us and should return an ROI of 154% within 2 years

Five rules for logical grouping storylines

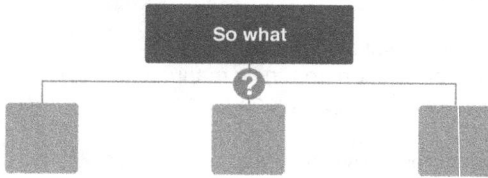

1   **Taken together** the ideas pass the MECE test (the ideas are Mutually Exclusive and Collectively Exhaustive, or in simpler terms there are no overlaps and no gaps in the thinking).

Individually each idea:

2   provokes or responds to just one question in the audience's mind

3   synthesises or summarises the ideas below

4   parents 2 to 5 mini-ideas

5   adds genuine value to the story.

To test whether the supporting ideas you have presented are strong enough to make your case, you will want to ask yourself whether your grouping meets the following five structural tests:

1   **Together, the supporting ideas in the storyline must pass the 'MECE test'.** * This is both one of the hardest and one of the most useful of the tests. Here is a simple example: when presented with the following list, you would easily recognise that one item does not belong:

- kangaroo
- koala bear
- echidna
- fish
- wallaby

All of these items except one – fish – are Australian mammals. This is easy to spot, but this is a much harder test to use when evaluating business storylines containing complex ideas. It is, however, a very useful test.

---

*   'MECE' is a term that was discussed extensively by Barbara Minto in her book *The Minto Pyramid Principle*. The term, however, goes back much further than the 1960s. It goes back to John Duns Scotus, a philosopher from the Middle Ages who wrote about the way of distinguishing between things. Some folk prefer a simpler acronym that has the same meaning: NONG. This stands for 'no overlaps, no gaps'.

2   **Each supporting idea must provoke and respond to just one question in the audience's mind.** A simple day-to-day example helps explain this concept.

Imagine yourself talking to a friend. You might say something simple like: 'We should have dinner on Saturday night'. In putting forward this proposition you are expecting your friend will say something like: 'Great, where should we go?', inviting you to offer a range of potential restaurants. It's obvious that you would not start providing lots of reasons why you should go out to dinner if your friend has agreed it's a great idea.

It's the same with each of your supporting ideas. You must invite your audience to ask a question that you can then answer. The challenge is to anticipate what that question will be and respond accordingly without actually being face to face with your audience. You might need to rely on others to help you understand your audience and also make a series of assumptions. It's also challenging as you will still be clarifying your thinking and distilling your ideas while you prepare the storyline.

3   **Each supporting idea must synthesise or summarise the ideas under it.** This is critical. Until you get to the bottom of your storyline, each supporting idea in a grouping structure parents a group of subordinate ideas, and each idea at the top must either summarise or synthesise the ideas below it. Here's how to differentiate between **summary** and **synthesis**:

—   *Summary:* describes a set of data. For example: 'All Australian surfboards are great to surf with.'*

—   *Synthesis:* explains what the set of data means. For example: 'When choosing a new surfboard, you must choose an Australian board as they are the best.'

4   **Each supporting idea must parent two to five subordinate ideas.** This is a simple rule but highly effective for pruning and for pushing your thinking. If you've come up with a long list of supporting ideas, it's time to sit back and either discard some or identify themes that could tie the supporting ideas together.

---

*   This assertion is based on national pride and absolutely no knowledge of surfing! It is an illustration only.

For example, in coming up with a list of seven different types of surfboard, you might group them according to length, style or perhaps according to price. The trick is to work out the best way to organise the ideas that will resonate with your audience while also supporting your message.

5   **Each supporting idea must add genuine value to the story.**
There is no point including ideas just to pad your story out rather than helping you inform or persuade your audience. In particular, be wary of including information that only demonstrates how much has been done, rather than providing insights that support your 'So what'. Be ruthless!

The deductive structure (enables you to explain why, what and how in one storyline)

A **deductive structure** enables you to build a case for a specific course of action by wrapping *why something should be done* and *how it should be done* into the one storyline.* It takes the audience on the journey.

In a deductive structure there are two supporting points, represented by the arrow-shaped boxes that lead you to the third point, which is your recommended action. (Compare this to the earlier image for the grouping structure, in which the supporting ideas are in rectangular and not arrow-shaped boxes.) At the simplest level, here is what a deductive storyline looks like:

Deductive storyline

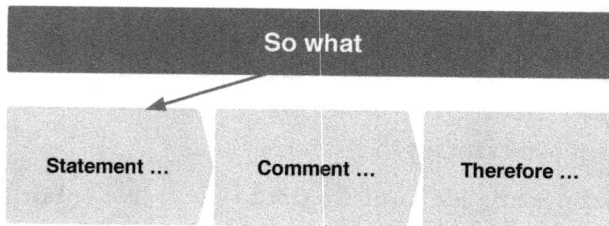

---

*   Storylining logic is based on classical logic but adjusted to suit a communication context rather than a problem solving – or 'prove it is so' – context. For example, classical logic would say that Socrates is a man, all men are mortal, therefore Socrates is mortal. However, storylining logic would want to see actions in the 'therefore' point. It, therefore, requires a different approach. Storylining logic would follow a pattern like this: all men in our group must have beards, Socrates is a clean-shaven man who wants to join our group, therefore Socrates must grow a beard.

You might choose this structure for SurfCo's leadership if you needed to persuade them that Swell Boards was the right investment to make *while also* gaining their agreement on a detailed negotiation plan. Here's an example of what that storyline might look like.

Deductive storyline: SurfCo example

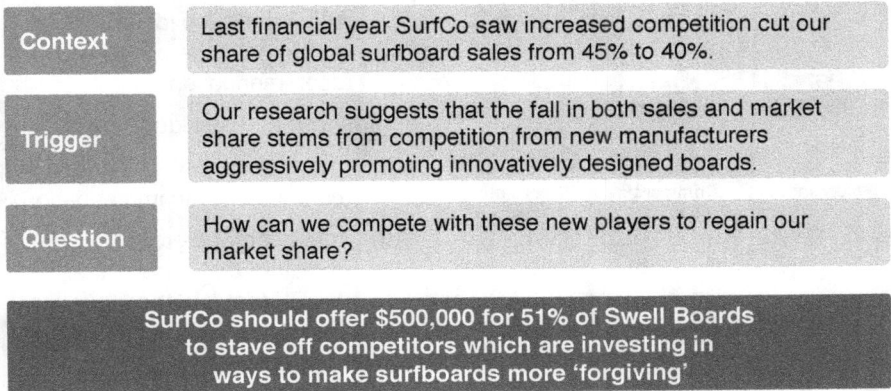

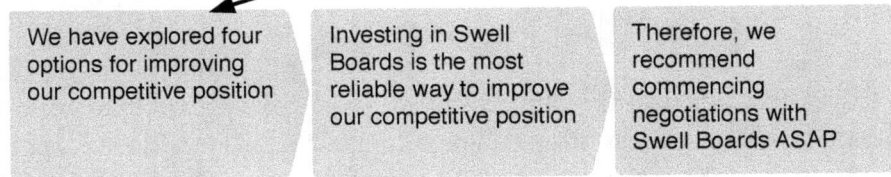

Context	Last financial year SurfCo saw increased competition cut our share of global surfboard sales from 45% to 40%.
Trigger	Our research suggests that the fall in both sales and market share stems from competition from new manufacturers aggressively promoting innovatively designed boards.
Question	How can we compete with these new players to regain our market share?

SurfCo should offer $500,000 for 51% of Swell Boards to stave off competitors which are investing in ways to make surfboards more 'forgiving'

We have explored four options for improving our competitive position	Investing in Swell Boards is the most reliable way to improve our competitive position	Therefore, we recommend commencing negotiations with Swell Boards ASAP
• Developing new surfboard features ourselves • Poaching a team of surfboard innovators from a competitor such as 1, 2 or 3 • Investing in an innovative surfboard manufacturer such as Swell Boards, SurFree or three other earlier stage groups • Buying an innovative surfboard manufacturer outright	• Investing in Swell Boards is the start-up investment most likely to improve our competitive position • Developing our own board features would take too long and be too expensive to take on competitors • Poaching a team of surfboard innovators is risky and expensive • Buying an innovative surfboard manufacturer outright is problematic because those that are for sale have uncommercial ideas	• Agree who should run the process from our end • Map out our negotiation strategy, including what is on the table and what is not • Get legal and financial advice re: that strategy • Agree our internal timeframes

In this deductive storyline the first arrow-shaped box lays out the options, the second analyses which is best (no doubt against a set of criteria such as profitability, technology and ease of executing the deal), and the third section lays out the action required to make it all happen.

Four rules for deductive storylines

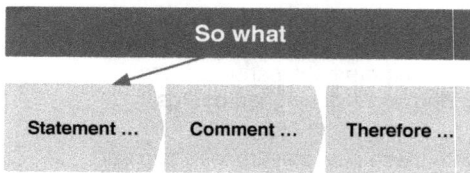

1 **As a whole** the ideas lead to only one possible recommendation.

Individually each idea:

2 must do its 'job' as a statement, comment or recommendation

3 must parent a grouping structure that passes the MECE test (i.e. the ideas are mutually exclusive, collectively exhaustive)

4 add genuine value to the story.

To test whether the supporting ideas you have presented in a deductive structure are strong enough to convince your audience, ask yourself whether your structure meets the following four structural tests:

1 **As a whole, the supporting ideas must lead to only one possible recommendation.** This means that the first two points – which are the 'statement' and the 'comment'– lead to one, and only one, possible recommendation, which is the 'therefore' point.

2 **Each supporting idea must do its 'job' as a 'statement', 'comment' or 'therefore'.** Unlike in a grouping structure, each top-level supporting idea has a unique role to play within the storyline:

   – *Statement:* This is something new to the audience that lays the foundation for the story to come. It may set up a series of conditions to be met, define a problem that must be solved, or explain criteria for success.

— *Comment:* This must comment on the statement in such a way that it is tightly connected to it. If the connection to the statement is weak, the storyline will fail. It will often begin with either the word 'however' or 'but'.

— *Therefore:* This must be the only natural action that you could recommend if the first two points hold true and the links between them also hold true.

This is where storylines use deductive logic differently compared to classical problem solving. In storylining, we use deduction to drive towards the only logical action that arises out of the combination of the 'statement' and the 'comment'. We lead towards an action plan rather than proof that something is correct.* Here are two examples to illustrate – one that does not work and one that does:

> *This chain does not present a logical flow:*
>
> **Statement:** Top surfers are incredibly fit.
> **Comment:** You are not fit.
> **Therefore:** Therefore, you should get fit.

> *This chain does present a logical flow:*
>
> **Statement:** All top surfers are incredibly fit.
> **Comment:** You want to be a top surfer but are not incredibly fit.
> **Therefore:** Therefore, you need to become incredibly fit.

Although the recommendation is close to being right in the first example (it recommends getting fit, not 'incredibly fit'), the first two points are not sufficiently tightly connected to lead to that being the right recommendation. And it's also not clear that you want to be a top surfer.

---

* If you want to learn more about classical logic, you may find Marianne Talbot from Oxford University to be a terrific teacher in this area. Her iTunes University modules are informative and clear – and free.

3   **Each supporting idea must parent a grouping structure that passes the MECE test (see above).** This is for two essential reasons:

–   Deductive storylines are potentially fragile: if one of the links between the ideas in the chain breaks, the recommendation becomes irrelevant. Stacking a deductive chain underneath, say, the statement would put the statement at risk of failure if the connections between the lower-level chain broke. In contrast, the grouping structure is much more robust.

–   Deductive chains require patience from your audience to work through the reasoning before they get to the actions. Asking your audience to read or listen through a number of chains layered onto each other would be confusing.

That said, if you get a deductive storyline right it can be very powerful.

4   **Each supporting idea must add genuine value to the story.** Don't include ideas just to pad your story out. Only include ideas that help you inform or persuade your audience.

HOW TO TEST IF YOUR STORYLINE IS FIT FOR PURPOSE

The most critical skill for creating consistently strong storylines is to stick to the storyline rules. The rules are not an end in themselves – they flush out the things that really matter and fundamentally drive clear thinking. They help you find the ideas that will answer the question your audience wants answered rather than just focusing on what you want to talk about. They also help you test whether your argument 'stacks up' and that your point of view is supported by ideas that are logically robust.

Identifying anywhere that your storyline is weak or does not have a logical flow is a great way to discover what further work needs to be done. So, here is our 10-Point Storyline Test that ties all the rules together. We find it to be highly useful in measuring how robust the thinking is within business communication. A score of less than 7 out of 10 on this test would indicate that more work must be done, and you should really be aiming for a 10 out of 10. Try this on one of your storylines to test how strong it is. Or, better still, ask someone else to test your storyline!

The 10-Point Storyline Test drives quality of thinking

Is the introduction right?

1. Is the context right – does the storyline start in the right place in time? ☐

2. Does the trigger describe why you are communicating with this audience now? ☐

3. Is the question really the single question we want to answer? ☐

Is there one clear, powerful statement of the 'So what'?

4. Is there one clear 'So what' that is 25 words or less? ☐

5. Is it powerful – does it summarise or ideally synthesise? ☐

Is the supporting storyline robust?

6. Is the top-line support for the 'So what' logically sound – grouping or deductive? ☐

7. Are the second and third level supports logically sound – grouping or deductive? ☐

8. Is the storyline MECE (categorised well and enough evidence) at every level? ☐

Does it meet the audience needs?

9. Does it meet the audience's needs and concerns? ☐

10. Does it suit their 'style' – type and level of support? ☐

Total / 10 ☐

The value of testing a storyline

This all came into play strongly when we were working with a client recently.

They had prepared an important and hard-won presentation for a potential partner using what they thought was a well-structured storyline. The ideas in the grouping structure were tight, and the presentation pack was organised according to that grouping structure. The content was broadly on point.

However, the presentation itself was a disaster, and the team managed to get a key influencer off side very quickly. When using our 10-point test to debrief, they realised that they had oriented the question from *their point of view*, not their *audience's point of view*. They had asked, 'Why should we partner with this prospect?', rather than 'Why should this prospect partner with us?'

When recrafting the communication for future pitches, they had a very different story that was better targeted and more specific, relevant and powerful.

* * * * *

As you learn more about the rules that hold storylines together, you will see they become a bit like Lego: so long as the connectors 'fit', you can move things around and create highly nuanced structures. For beginner storyliners there are the simple blocks in primary colours to build with that allow you to create all kinds of structures that are fun to play with. For more advanced storyliners, there are the custom bricks that fit together in all sorts of clever ways to build magnificent structures that are as fancy as Star Wars battleships – but better because you have designed them yourself.

Now that you understand what storylines are, how they work and the many benefits of using them, let's look at the seven classic business storylines that will help you in your business communication. These are the different patterns that will form your storylining toolkit.

THREE

MASTERING THE SEVEN CLASSIC BUSINESS STORYLINE PATTERNS

So, now you know about the benefits of storylines and how they work, it's time to start thinking about putting them into practice. One question we often hear at this point is, 'Do you have to start from scratch and come up with a storyline for each new communication?' The answer is *no*. You can use a 'storyline pattern' to kick-start the process.

Let's see how this works …

People often talk about the seven great story structures, which include the comedy, the tragedy and the hero's journey. Well, in business – as we have said – we think there are also underlying patterns in business communication.

In this chapter we are going to examine our seven classic storyline patterns that will help you communicate your ideas in a way that is both clear and compelling. We'll explain how they work, when you should use each one, and the benefits of each approach, and we'll provide an example of each storyline in action.* Master these and you will be well on the way to becoming a great business communicator.

We won't make you wait any longer. Here they are! The seven classic business storyline patterns are:

Grouping storylines

1   *Action Jackson* – for action plans.

2   *The Pitch* – for pitches and proposals.

3   *Traffic Light* – for updates.

Deductive storylines

4   *Close the Gap* – for improvement recommendations.

5   *Houston, We Have a Problem* – for explaining how to solve problems.

6   *To B or Not to B* – for explaining which option is best.

7   *Watch Out* – to counter emerging risks.

So, let's find out how each of them works ...

---

*   These are examples that we have distilled from our experience and sanitised to protect the innocent, disguising names, companies and individuals as well as any figures. That said, these examples are from real experience. We've created these examples by focusing on generalities and structure and without being experts in each subject area. If you know more about the subject of a storyline than we do and think any of the content isn't quite right, please let us know so we can improve it for the next edition.

Pointers for picking and populating storyline patterns

Picking and populating a pattern can be faster and easier than starting from scratch, so we encourage you to look at our patterns at an early stage when developing your communication to see which one will best fit your circumstances. There are many ways to do this. You may like to scan the patterns to see which one 'feels right', or alternatively you may like to step back for a moment and think about your audience's needs first.

If your audience needs to know only why *or* how – or potentially *what* – needs to be done in one piece of communication, a **grouping structure** will work best. If your audience needs to know both why *and* how something should be done in one communication, you will need a **deductive storyline**.

If you're not sure, brainstorm with your colleagues to flush out your ideas further before you decide. This step will also help you clarify if you have all the information you need.

Whatever your tactic, pick a pattern that fits best and sketch your ideas into it, being mindful of the critical role each element of the storyline plays as you go.

Be careful here. Do not force fit your thinking into the pattern and sacrifice its logical integrity. If one of the patterns is not right, you may need to look for another one or potentially start building your storyline from scratch.

Whichever way you go, keep coming back to the 10-point test to keep yourself on track.

THESE THREE POWERFUL PATTERNS WILL HELP YOU USE GROUPINGS

Action Jackson for action plans

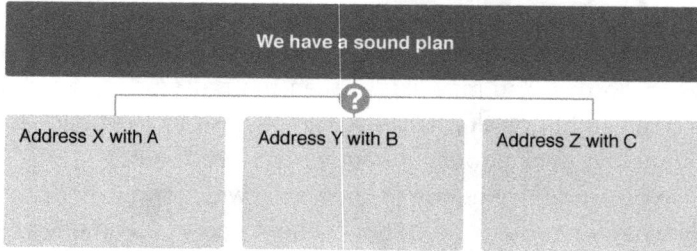

We have a sound plan		
Address X with A	Address Y with B	Address Z with C

The Pitch for proposals and recommendations

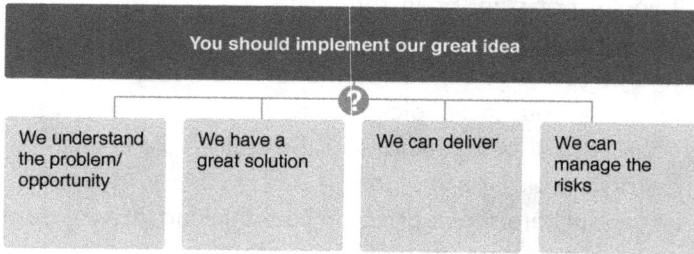

You should implement our great idea			
We understand the problem/ opportunity	We have a great solution	We can deliver	We can manage the risks

Traffic Light for updates and compliance stories

Overall we're on track		
We have completed X	We have started Y	We have a clear pathway to deliver remaining tasks on time

THE FOUR TOP DEDUCTIVE PATTERNS MAKE STORYLINING EASIER

Close the Gap for improvement recommendations

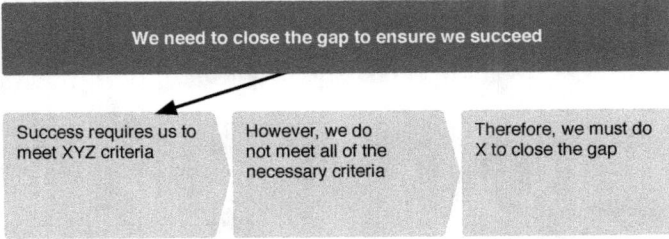

We need to close the gap to ensure we succeed

| Success requires us to meet XYZ criteria | However, we do not meet all of the necessary criteria | Therefore, we must do X to close the gap |

Houston, We Have a Problem for explaining how to solve problems

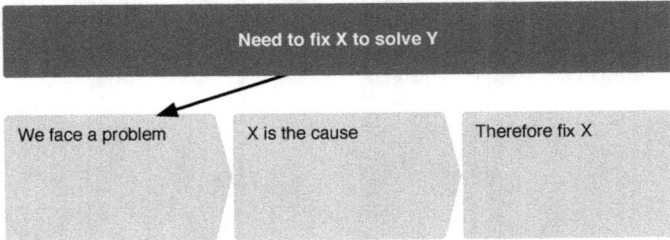

Need to fix X to solve Y

| We face a problem | X is the cause | Therefore fix X |

To B or Not to B for explaining which option is best

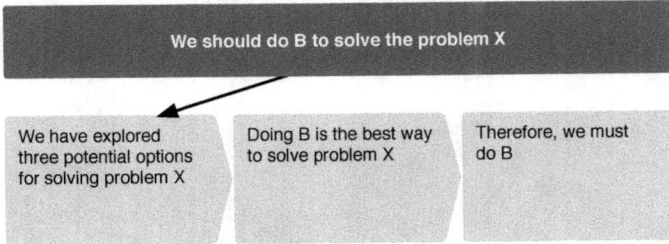

We should do B to solve the problem X

| We have explored three potential options for solving problem X | Doing B is the best way to solve problem X | Therefore, we must do B |

Watch Out to counter emerging risks

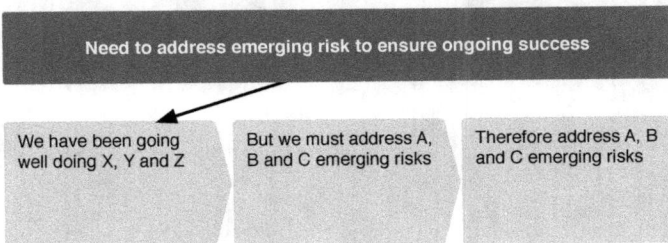

Need to address emerging risk to ensure ongoing success

| We have been going well doing X, Y and Z | But we must address A, B and C emerging risks | Therefore address A, B and C emerging risks |

GROUPING STORYLINES

1　**Action Jackson** – for action plans.
2　**The Pitch** – for pitches and proposals.
3　**Traffic Light** – for updates.

ACTION JACKSON – FOR ACTION PLANS

Sometimes we don't have to argue a case about *why* we have to act – we just have to act! That's where Action Jackson comes in. It's an action storyline, pure and simple. Action Jackson tells the audience what steps are required to implement a particular action.

To make Action Jackson work for you:

- understand that it's a simple storyline describing steps

- use it when you want to spell out an action plan

- build it to map an overall recommendation and supporting steps

- avoid using it when your audience still needs to be convinced.

Let's discuss each of these below.

Understand that Action Jackson is a simple storyline describing steps

Action Jackson couldn't be simpler! It describes actions to audiences who do not need to be persuaded, usually because they already know why something needs to be done – either it's obvious to them or they have endorsed the recommendation previously.

Let's have a look at the Action Jackson storyline.

Action Jackson pattern

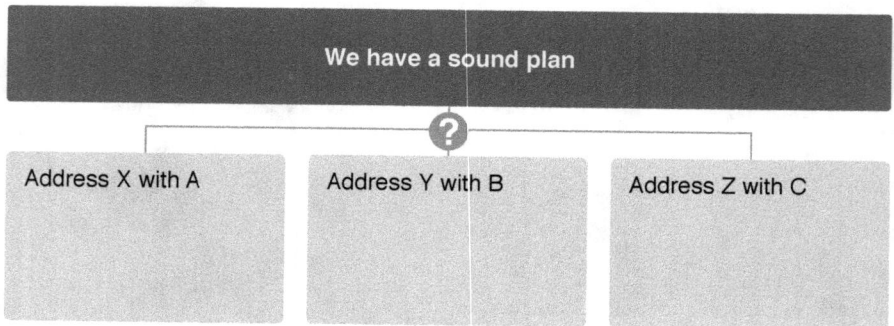

We have a sound plan		
Address X with A	Address Y with B	Address Z with C

Use Action Jackson when you want to spell out an action plan

You would choose the Action Jackson storyline when you need to outline the steps you will be taking to implement a recommendation.

Like many of our other classic storylines, this might be when you need to present a paper to a senior team or a board when they need to understand how a particular strategy needs to be implemented. Or it could be the structure for a briefing in a team meeting, such as a routine team huddle.

Either way, the audience must already be convinced that action is necessary and be curious about what specific actions you are recommending.

Let's look at two examples. When thinking about how these structures might be used, we think about the 'macro' level and the 'micro' level. Macro refers to larger – often high stakes – pieces of communication, and micro is smaller, day-to-day communication. In both situations the logic must be strong and the presentation powerful.

Example: the recovery plan

Action Jackson is a great storyline structure when you don't have to convince your audience on a course of action, you only need to outline *how you will make it happen*. For example, the finance team in a large bank used the Action Jackson pattern when they had already made the case that a business unit was missing their stretch target and they wanted to explain what steps they could take to make up the shortfall.

You can see in the storyline on the following page that the context and trigger remind the audience of what had already been agreed. The core of the storyline outlines the steps required to close the shortfall, and then the next level of support outlines the actions required to implement each step.

The team mapped their ideas into the storyline on a whiteboard before preparing their PowerPoint pack. The pack itself had substantially more detail than this high-level storyline as the team expected the leadership to drill down into the specifics around how they could increase their service fees without upsetting their customer base and their marketing messaging.

The Friendly Bank storyline

Context	The Friendly Bank (Friendly) was set a $100M stretch target in December
Trigger	Finance has been analysing forecasts to understand whether Friendly can achieve target and found Friendly needs to identify initiatives to close out a potential $1M shortfall
Question	How can Friendly close out the shortfall?

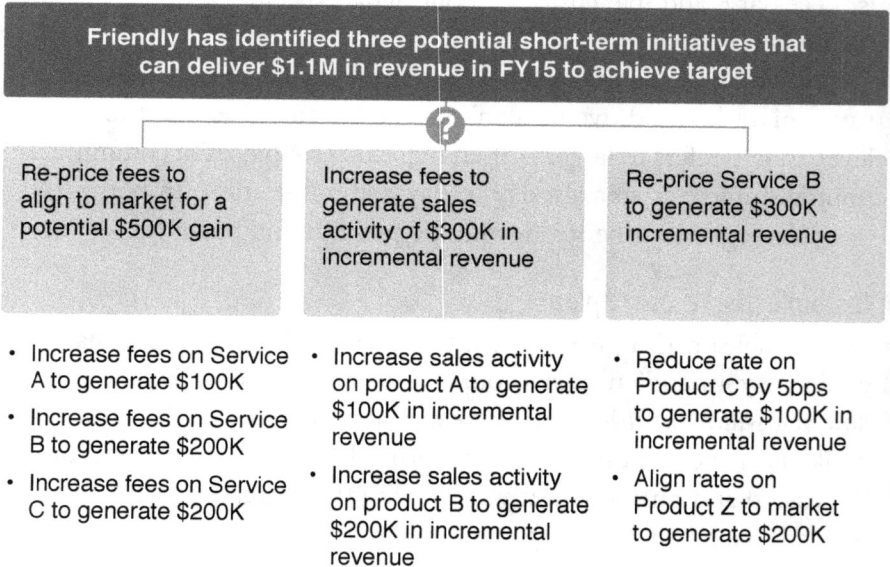

Friendly has identified three potential short-term initiatives that can deliver $1.1M in revenue in FY15 to achieve target

Re-price fees to align to market for a potential $500K gain	Increase fees to generate sales activity of $300K in incremental revenue	Re-price Service B to generate $300K incremental revenue
• Increase fees on Service A to generate $100K • Increase fees on Service B to generate $200K • Increase fees on Service C to generate $200K	• Increase sales activity on product A to generate $100K in incremental revenue • Increase sales activity on product B to generate $200K in incremental revenue	• Reduce rate on Product C by 5bps to generate $100K in incremental revenue • Align rates on Product Z to market to generate $200K

Working through the storyline together in advance allowed the team to test the thinking and think through the tough questions they might be asked. From this, they fine-tuned their answers. This is a powerful way to use storylining to help push your thinking and refine your communication.

Example: the verbal team briefing

Action Jackson is a great storyline structure for short, sharp team briefings.

For example, one of the teams we were supporting needed to provide an update for a senior executive. The team needed to explain the implementation plan for deploying the new system (NewSys) that would take over some of the manual data-handling aspects of their job and underpin the shift in the team's role from being technical experts to business advisers and partners. The storyline below was used to provide a quick snapshot on implementation as part of a verbal progress update.

Transformation storyline

Context	In January we updated you on our team transformation and outlined our strategy and proposed plan
Trigger	Since January we have moved well down the implementation path
Question	How has your implementation proceeded?

The Transformation program is enabling the team to shift from being technical experts to being advisers who partner with the business to solve critical problems

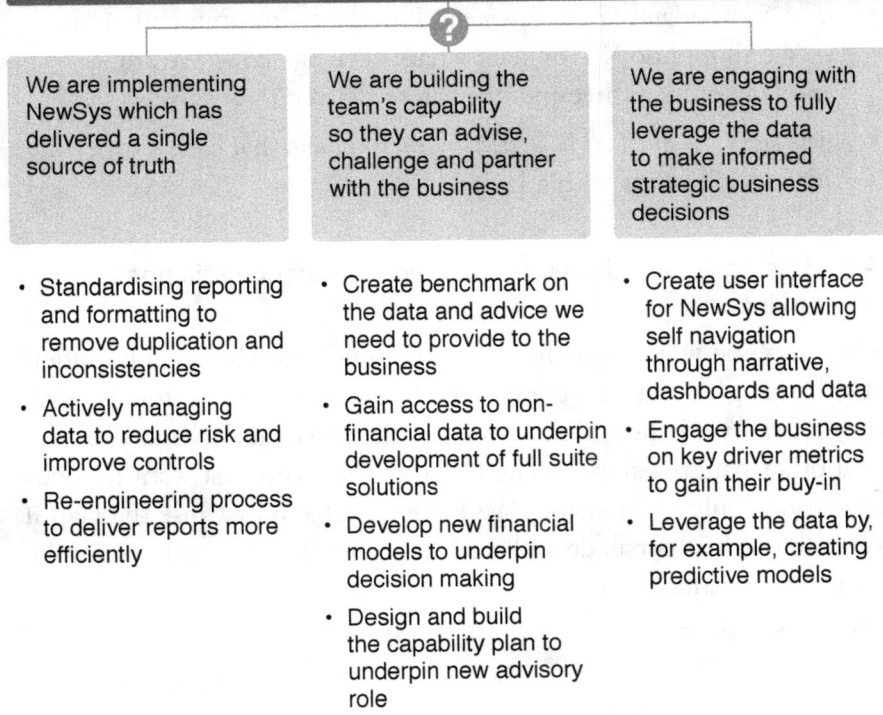

We are implementing NewSys which has delivered a single source of truth	We are building the team's capability so they can advise, challenge and partner with the business	We are engaging with the business to fully leverage the data to make informed strategic business decisions
• Standardising reporting and formatting to remove duplication and inconsistencies	• Create benchmark on the data and advice we need to provide to the business	• Create user interface for NewSys allowing self navigation through narrative, dashboards and data
• Actively managing data to reduce risk and improve controls	• Gain access to non-financial data to underpin development of full suite solutions	• Engage the business on key driver metrics to gain their buy-in
• Re-engineering process to deliver reports more efficiently	• Develop new financial models to underpin decision making	• Leverage the data by, for example, creating predictive models
	• Design and build the capability plan to underpin new advisory role	

The team mapped out the story visually, as the one-pager provided a handy reference during the conversation, both for themselves and for the executive. They chose not to prepare a more substantial document to accompany the storyline given there were few contentious issues, the project was on track, and they expected the executive to want to know more about the project rather than challenge it.

Build Action Jackson to map an overall recommendation and supporting steps

There are some key elements you must get right and some traps to avoid:

- *The introduction (the CTQ ... the 'context', 'trigger' and 'question') must lead to actions* – it should remind the audience about what has already been agreed and lead to a 'how' question. But, be careful to test that the audience really does need an Action Jackson storyline and does not need convincing about *why* action is needed or *why* certain steps are required. If that were the case, you would use the Close the Gap pattern (which we look at next).

- *The 'So what' must be a statement.* It may be a recommendation – 'We should do X' – or state what's been agreed – 'We are implementing a three-month plan to deliver Y'.

- *The storyline must all be actions,* which means that each supporting idea ideally starts with a verb.

Avoid using Action Jackson when your audience still needs to be convinced

This storyline will only help you with audiences who already understand and agree that the action you are recommending is important. If they do not yet believe that, this is *not* the storyline for you. You may find other patterns such as The Pitch useful if you first want to focus on reasons only, or Houston, We Have a Problem or Close the Gap if you want to first persuade and then run through the action plan in the same conversation.

THE PITCH – FOR PITCHES AND PROPOSALS

An often-quoted maxim is that *why* is more important than *how*. If you have not persuaded your audience – your team, your boss, anyone really – *why* something should be done then don't tell them *how to do it*. They just won't see the point. That's where The Pitch comes in.

The Pitch enables you to explain why your idea is a good one, whether it's to collaborate on a project, implement a new approach, or invest in a new business. It provides a clear and straightforward pattern to gain your audience's attention and then persuade them with a series of compelling reasons why they should agree with you.

To make this pattern work for you, you must:

- know that The Pitch articulates and supports a recommendation
- use The Pitch when you need to persuade someone
- understand that The Pitch highlights your value proposition 'right up front'
- avoid being glib; it's critical that your supporting reasons convince your audience.

Let's discuss each in turn.

Understand that The Pitch articulates and supports a recommendation

Here's how The Pitch works.

The Pitch pattern

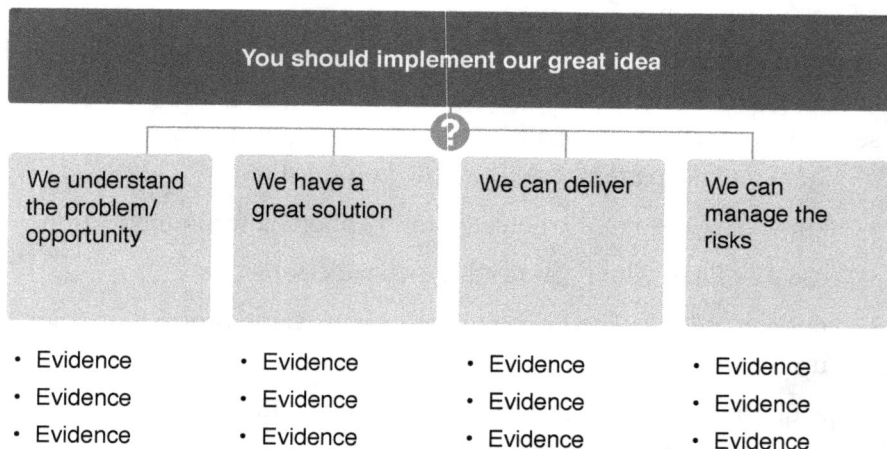

You should implement our great idea			
We understand the problem/ opportunity	We have a great solution	We can deliver	We can manage the risks
• Evidence	• Evidence	• Evidence	• Evidence
• Evidence	• Evidence	• Evidence	• Evidence
• Evidence	• Evidence	• Evidence	• Evidence

Use The Pitch when you need to persuade someone

Persuasion is both a science and an art. Storylining science can help you map out the complex ideas you must communicate clearly, and the art is to present those in a way that is truly compelling, whatever the context and whomever the audience.

If you need to persuade your team that something non-controversial is important, you usually need more science than art. They know you, you know them, and all you need to do is map out the ideas clearly to avoid ambiguity or rambling.

If, however, you need to persuade someone you don't know to take a leap of faith, you'll need a strong blend of both science and art. In these situations, map out your ideas carefully with your audience in mind and pay extra attention to who presents, how they do it, and how much they invest in rehearsing.

Let's look at how The Pitch can help.

Example: the big pitch

We nearly always use this approach when helping our clients to prepare proposals. These can be pitches for sales of many kinds, or in some case we've helped clients 'pitch' for senior roles, such as C-suite positions.

A recent case where we helped a technology company pitch a partnership idea to a telecommunications company is a terrific example of the effectiveness of this storyline. It was a high-stakes pitch: the technology company needed to not only engage the prospect but to do so quickly so they could beat their competition, who also wanted to partner with the telco. The telco would only go with one of them.

At least one member of the decision-making team at the telco would need to be persuaded of the general merits of the proposal as well as the merits of the type of network they were recommending, as that person was wedded to a different type of network. The team's greatest fear was getting this influential person off side, which would scupper the whole deal.

As a result, the team invested significant energy in getting the messaging right for the first and second sections of the story, where they tailored the benefits to specifically address this stakeholder's concerns as well as those of the other decision makers.

They also needed the prospect to be confident that engaging in the partnership was low risk.

The storyline is on the following page.

The Telco Pitch storyline

Context	We are one of the top in our field globally and our success depends upon successful partnerships with groups like yours

Trigger	We would like to establish a mutually beneficial partnership with you

Question	Why should we partner with you?

Joining forces would lead to a powerful partnership that benefits both of us

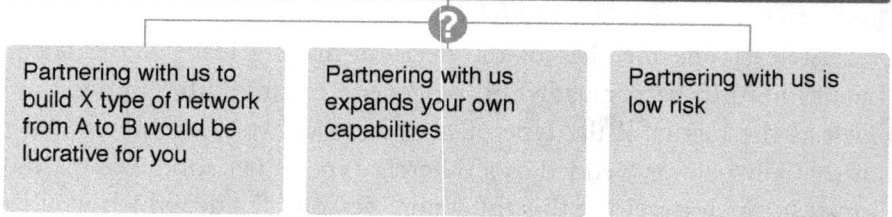

Partnering with us to build X type of network from A to B would be lucrative for you	Partnering with us expands your own capabilities	Partnering with us is low risk

- We will invest by building X type of network from A to B
- We will pay you to manage the network
- We will pay you for your licence to operate the network

- We will strengthen your competitive position in the market by helping you get ahead of your competitors
- We will help you prepare for the future by broadening the types of networks you operate and services you offer your customers
- We will train your people to manage the network

- We offer you exclusive use of the network outside our own needs
- We have a successful track record of partnering with companies like yours
- We have a vested interest in the relationship being successful

Example: persuading your team

Once you have decided that something simple and straightforward should be done, all you want to do is make it happen. However, getting it done often means you need to persuade others before work can begin.

Here's a story that a client of ours used to persuade a leader to allow a reporting team to implement a new analytics tool to prepare high-stakes reports.

Although this is a simple story on the surface, this client had been struggling for some time to persuade the leader to allow the change. The leader was adamant he did not want the process for creating this particular report to change as this was the most critical report he presented to the CEO each month, and any errors would affect his credibility.

Given previous attempts had failed, our client went to the effort of mapping the ideas out on a page to increase his confidence in his messaging. The storyline is shown on the next page.

The 'new way' Pitch storyline

Context	I am aware how sensitive the Alpha report is and how essential it is for the numbers to be rock solid each month
Trigger	Since we spoke last we have successfully introduced the 'new way' on a range of other sensitive reports and would like to talk through a careful way of introducing the 'new way' for the Alpha report
Question	How can you be certain that the 'new way' will ensure the numbers are rock solid?

Introducing the 'new way' for preparing the Alpha report is low risk, efficient and essential

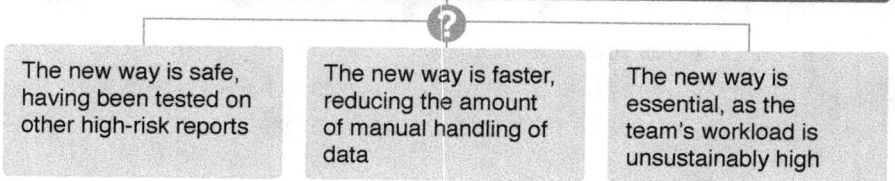

The new way is safe, having been tested on other high-risk reports	The new way is faster, reducing the amount of manual handling of data	The new way is essential, as the team's workload is unsustainably high
• We have been successfully using the new way to prepare X and Y reports for three months now • We have been successfully using the new way to prepare Z report for one month	• Previously we gathered the data from multiple sources and crunched the numbers manually, which is time consuming and risky • The 'new way' involves running automated reports in the new system, less numbers to crunch manually and more time to test the results	• The team now prepares 5 more reports each month than they prepared 3 months ago • One of the 5 team members will leave at the end of the month and will not be replaced due to the hiring freeze • The team appears stretched which creates more risk: 2 were each off for 3 days last month with flu, another is also unwell, and morale is falling

The good news is that in thinking through and being articulate about the senior leader's sensitivities, our client was persuasive and the 'new way' was implemented.

Understand that The Pitch highlights your value proposition 'right up front'

The Pitch is structurally simple but critically dependent upon getting the introductory flow right so you focus on the points that matter to your audience. Working through each element of the storylining process is critical to create a powerful, on-point pitch. Here are some things you must do:

- *Sweat over the purpose and the audience* even though these will not be mapped out within your communication. What do you really want your audience to know, think or do, and who will make the decision? Be specific, test it with your colleagues, and make sure you nail this before you make your pitch. It's easy to get either or both wrong and to orient the pitch so it misses its target.

- *Sweat even more over the introduction.* Think very carefully about your context as the starting point for your story. In a pitch this very often describes the problem you are there to help your prospect address. For example, if you were improving the delivery speed from your warehouse you might say something like: 'customers in Quambatook must currently wait five to seven days to receive their order even though the Mallee distribution centre is only two hours away'. This is much better than something general like: 'Quambatook customers have been complaining of slow delivery'.

- *Ensure your answer ('So what') is powerful and persuasive.* This is where you grab their attention with your value proposition. It must be crafted to give your audience confidence that you know exactly how to help them fix their problem.

- *Support your answer with three to five powerful, bespoke reasons* as to why they should 'buy your proposition'. These must be mutually exclusive and collectively exhaustive – from your audience's perspective. They must also be ordered in a way that will be sensible to your audience – this most likely means placing the element that will benefit the audience the most first.

Any pitch – whatever structure you use – must 'pop'. You need to show the right amount of passion, be on point, and present professionally. The Pitch storyline helps you stay on point. We'll leave the passion and presentation to you!

Avoid being glib; it's critical that your story convinces your audience

We have described The Pitch as a simple structure, but that simplicity is deceptive. It's critical that your points are tailored to address your audience's specific concerns both in terms of language and substance.

If you are not careful, you may come across as superficial, or worse, glib. So, take the time to sweat the ideas that belong in the pitch so that they are powerful and targeted *at your audience's needs*, not primarily *at your own needs*. In other words, explain why they should partner with you, or how your idea will benefit them, or why your solution is the best option ... not just how it will benefit you.

TRAFFIC LIGHT – FOR UPDATES

Every business, every project, every team and every individual professional needs to update others on their progress at some point. And
when we do, no matter how complex the scenario, the 'So what' can be
boiled down to one of three words: the status of red, amber or green.
Just like a traffic light. This pattern provides you with an easy way to
explain your status, whatever your colour.

To make the Traffic Light storyline work for you, you must:

- know that it provides a clear status update

- use it for status updates

- understand that it enables you to provide an overview – and as
  much detail as you want – to explain your current position

- avoid being sloppy.

We will now run through each of these points in more detail.

Understand that Traffic Light provides a clear status update

The Traffic Light storyline is a simple grouping. Importantly, it not only
provides a perspective on the key project elements, it also provides an
overall 'So what' on your progress.

Here's how Traffic Light works.

Traffic Light pattern

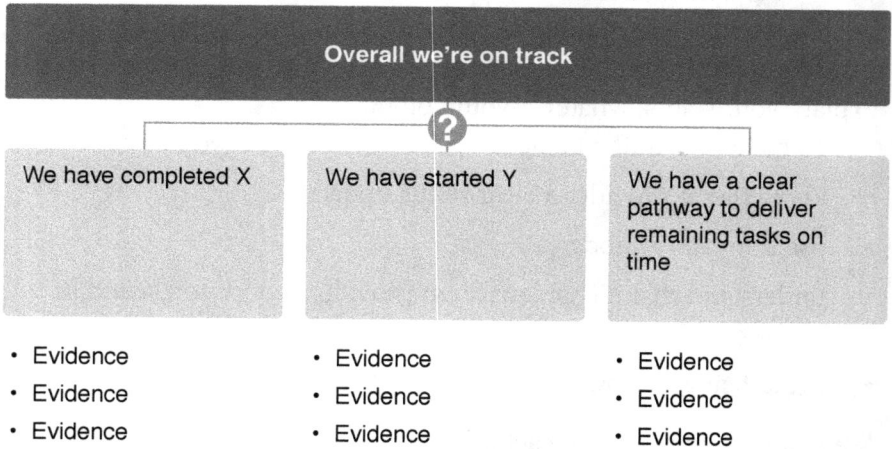

Overall we're on track		
We have completed X	We have started Y	We have a clear pathway to deliver remaining tasks on time

• Evidence	• Evidence	• Evidence
• Evidence	• Evidence	• Evidence
• Evidence	• Evidence	• Evidence

Use Traffic Light for status updates

This is a flexible pattern that enables you to describe where you are up to and why. It works for large, complex initiatives as well as simple ones. Here are two examples.

Example: updating about a large initiative

At the macro level you may update the leadership or perhaps even shareholders about the status of an initiative – such as a diversity program – across your whole organisation. You might, for example, prepare a PowerPoint presentation or an email that says something like the storyline on the following page.

Diversity storyline

Context	We are committed to increasing the diversity of our workforce
Trigger	Our most recent quarterly report is now in, showing our recent progress towards our diversity targets
Question	How are we tracking?

We are on track with meeting our 2017 diversity targets

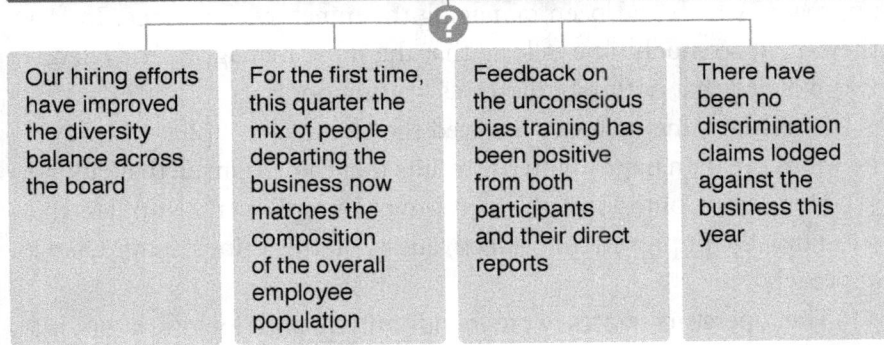

Our hiring efforts have improved the diversity balance across the board	For the first time, this quarter the mix of people departing the business now matches the composition of the overall employee population	Feedback on the unconscious bias training has been positive from both participants and their direct reports	There have been no discrimination claims lodged against the business this year

- 30% of our senior leadership team is now female and 20% of the team comes from a diverse ethnic background
- 60% of our new hires are female and 30% have diverse backgrounds

- The proportion of departures of both men and women came within 3% of the population
- The percentage of departures across all age brackets was within 5% of the population
- The proportion of departures across all other diversity categories was in proportion

- Leaders gave positive feedback, averaging 4.3 / 5
- Mid-level managers gave particularly strong feedback, averaging 4.8 / 5
- Team members gave positive feedback, averaging 4.2 / 5

- There have been no complaints about gender discrimination
- There have been no complaints about age-related discrimination
- There have been no complaints about race-based discrimination
- There have been no other kinds of discrimination complaints

Please note that this example is illustrative only. We recognise there are many kinds of diversity and that this is not a complete list.

Example: updating about an initiative

At the micro level you may describe the status of a local initiative that your team has undertaken; for example, reducing the time taken for top-priority maintenance issues to be addressed at a manufacturing plant.

The following example is from a consulting engagement at an outback mine site in Australia. The consulting team consisted of experienced mining hands who spent quite some time talking with the mine operators to work out the best ways to improve their maintenance approach, which had been damaging the mine's performance. In fact, they spent so much time talking that the mine manager – the client – was worried that nothing much was 'getting done'.

After the mine manager received the team's next update, however, he was more than happy with the results that came from all that talking.

Here is an outline of the deceptively simple verbal update that substantially improved the effectiveness of the mine's maintenance approach.

The operators' notes were hand-written and looked a bit like this (fleshed out more formally and with labels added for your easy reference):

Context: We are always looking for ways to improve our maintenance program.

Trigger: Working with ConsultCo over the past few weeks, we found a way to improve the maintenance program that will remove the bottlenecks within the mine.

Question: How will that work? (For speaker's reference only.)

Answer: We are changing the way we think and communicate about maintenance tasks to cut the risk of downtime, such as last month's major shutdown.

- We are now successfully prioritising maintenance tasks according to the impact on production rather than the time when the task was logged.

- We are continuing to improve communication between shift supervisors and the maintenance team by ensuring they discuss priorities at the start of each shift.

- We are working towards operators consistently telling supervisors as soon as they see a potential problem rather than waiting until something breaks.

Understand that Traffic Light enables you to provide a nuanced overview – and as much detail as you want – to explain your current position

Traffic Light allows you enormous flexibility to provide a nuanced 'So what' that is then supported by a list of reasons.

The strength of your storyline relies on thoughtful attention to the introduction. The introductory flow (the context, trigger and question) is key to this and enables you to assess whether you can 'cut, paste and tweak' from last time or whether you need to start from scratch. Thinking carefully about what really belongs in these introductory elements leads you to the right question – the one that your audience will really want to ask you this time.

Avoid being sloppy

Be careful with the Traffic Light pattern, as its flexibility can also be a weakness. Here are three critical things to avoid when using Traffic Light:

- *Avoid making assumptions about what your audience knows in relation to the issue.* You are in the business every day and are caught up in the detail, which makes it easy to miss external trends or themes that your leadership team may be across. Consider this when thinking through your introduction and the rest of the storyline.

- *Avoid automatically cutting and pasting from last time.* Given this will often be a routine update, it's all too easy to think 'things haven't changed much' and just update the numbers without thinking too hard. There are times when that is the right approach, but be careful not to make it your default position.

- *Avoid plonking your supporting ideas down without regard for the way they hang together.* It's easy to come up with a list of reasons why you think, for example, your risk management is in good shape. It's much harder to be confident that you have a complete set of reasons and then to order them intelligently.

DEDUCTIVE STORYLINES

CLOSE THE GAP – FOR IMPROVEMENT RECOMMENDATIONS

In business we are often asked to assess and address a gap between desired and actual performance. In these situations it can be tempting to focus only on where we want to go *or* where we are, rather than tightly linking the two. Our Close the Gap storyline enables you to provide clear and compelling reasoning as to why your plan is the right plan for closing the particular gap in question. It works particularly well when you know what success looks like, or what you need to do to comply with a set of regulations but you are not yet doing so.

To make Close the Gap work for you, you must:

- know that it explains where you are and where you need to get to

- use it to gain your audience's buy-in in one meeting

- build it to outline a case for your action plan

- stick to storylining rules so your audience supports your action plan.

We will now run through each of these points in more detail.

Understand that Close the Gap explains where you are and where you need to get to

Let's have a look at the Close the Gap storyline.

Close the Gap pattern

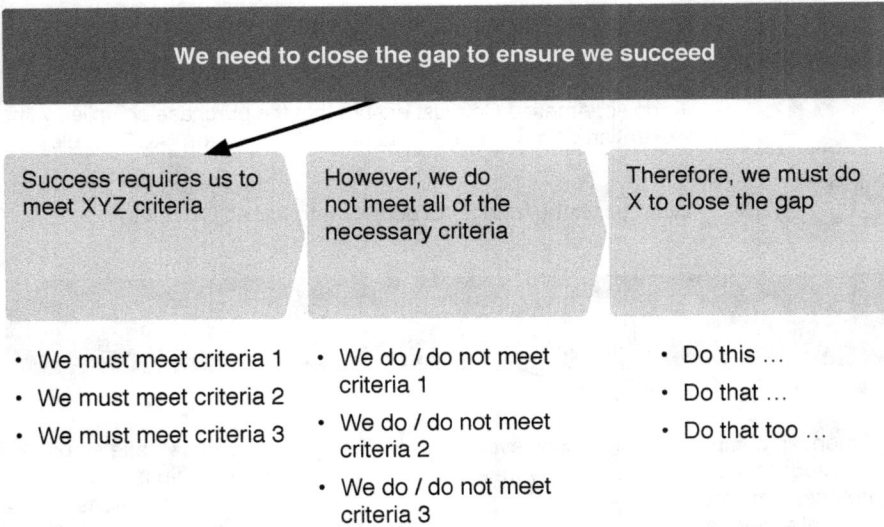

We need to close the gap to ensure we succeed

Success requires us to meet XYZ criteria	However, we do not meet all of the necessary criteria	Therefore, we must do X to close the gap
• We must meet criteria 1 • We must meet criteria 2 • We must meet criteria 3	• We do / do not meet criteria 1 • We do / do not meet criteria 2 • We do / do not meet criteria 3	• Do this ... • Do that ... • Do that too ...

Use Close the Gap to gain your audience's buy-in in one meeting

You would choose the Close the Gap storyline over Action Jackson when you need to educate your audience about what's required for success *at the same time as* providing the action plan. This might be when you need to present a paper to the board, to your leadership, or when you need a fast decision. You might also use it when you need to engage your team in both what needs to be done and why. Here are two examples to illustrate.

Example: entering a new market and due diligence

At the macro level, this storyline is powerful for business cases, legal advice, due diligence reports, audits and more. On the following page is an example.

Close the Gap was powerful when explaining to a US company how to tackle some of the legal aspects of entering the Australian market. If a US company wanted to make an asset purchase in Australia and needed information about three things – the intricacies of Australian Competition and Consumer Commission (ACCC) rules, how they are positioned in relation to these, and what they need to do to successfully purchase the asset – this would play out as shown overleaf.

America Co storyline

Context	America Co wants to purchase Australian mining company OzMines

Trigger	To do so, America Co must ensure that the purchase complies with Australian Competition & Consumer Commission (ACCC) rules

Question	What do we need to do to comply with the ACCC rules?

America Co needs to take steps to meet criteria X and Y to comply with the ACCC rules to qualify to purchase OzMines

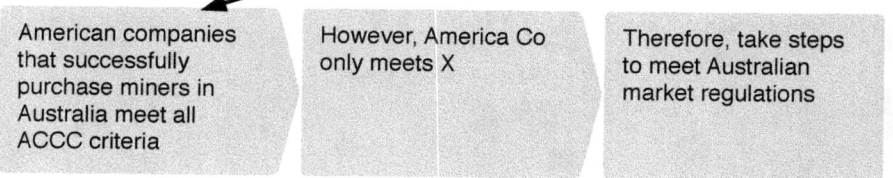

American companies that successfully purchase miners in Australia meet all ACCC criteria	However, America Co only meets X	Therefore, take steps to meet Australian market regulations
• We must meet criteria X • We must meet criteria Y • We must meet criteria Z	• America Co meets X • America Co does not meet Y • America Co may meet Z	• Do 1 to lock in X • Do 2 to meet Y • Do 3 to ensure Z is met

In this example, the legal team used the storyline to structure a letter of advice in a typical legal letter format and followed up with a phone call to work it through with the client and answer any questions. Given the client had expected there would be work for them to do to comply with the ACCC rules, it was a straightforward conversation that explained the rules they needed to comply with and the specific steps they needed to take.

Example: agile meetings

At the micro level this is one of the best 'stand up' storylines for the classic agile meeting.

Picture this: it's 9 am and you're about to host the stand up on the day's work. You need to explain to everyone what needs to be done to fix some problems that appeared in the team's model last week. The story might go like this:

Everyone, finishing Fred's model is a big priority, but given last week's distractions he won't be able to finish it by Friday on his own.

So, we need Mary and Jane to help Fred fix XYZ fields so the model can be delivered by Friday.

Here's why: for the model to be delivered by Friday, we need to have all XYZ fields complete. But, when we were testing it last night we found three of the fields had corrupted, so we need Mary and Jane to down tools on everything else and help Fred fix these three fields straight away.

Build Close the Gap to outline the case for your action plan

Close the Gap enables you to map out the criteria for success – however you define it – and then match your performance against this before articulating how to move closer towards your desired state.

Your criteria might be set by regulation, or by your own definition of what is required, and that you can persuade your audience is sensible. You then have an opportunity to comment on that in the second part of your structure by explaining how you or your business ranks against that criteria. The last section is, of course, to explain how you will close the gap between the initial criteria and your current state.

Stick to storylining rules so your audience supports your action plan

Here are some problems we often see with this storyline:

- *Having an incomplete or poorly organised set of criteria in the 'statement'.* If this set of criteria is incomplete or inaccurate the whole story will fall down.

- *Not linking the 'comment' tightly to the first statement.* If this connection is not tight, your audience will start debating with you and asking questions. They will also be less likely to enable you to get to your third point and support your action plan.

- *Not testing that the 'therefore' point flows naturally from the first two.* It may seem natural to you that your suggestion follows, but this is perhaps not the case for an outsider. We always recommend you ask a colleague to review your logic at a high level before you prepare your more detailed communication.

HOUSTON, WE HAVE A PROBLEM – FOR EXPLAINING HOW TO SOLVE PROBLEMS

When the crew on Apollo 13 uttered those now immortal words, 'Houston, we've had a problem', they didn't know they would become etched into the common vernacular. We use the phrase to describe one of the seven great business storylines, with a slight twist – we're talking about problems we 'have' now and what we're going to do about them.

Houston, We Have a Problem tells the audience about a business problem, its cause, and what steps are required to implement a recommended set of actions. It's a classic.

To make this pattern work for you, you must:

- understand that Houston is great at combining diagnostics and action
- use Houston when you must convince an audience of a problem and talk them through actions
- understand that Houston maps problems, the cause and resulting steps
- avoid overkill; Houston is about convincing.

Let's discuss each in turn.

Understand that Houston is great at combining diagnostics and action

Houston We Have a Problem is a simple deductive storyline.

Houston, We Have a Problem pattern

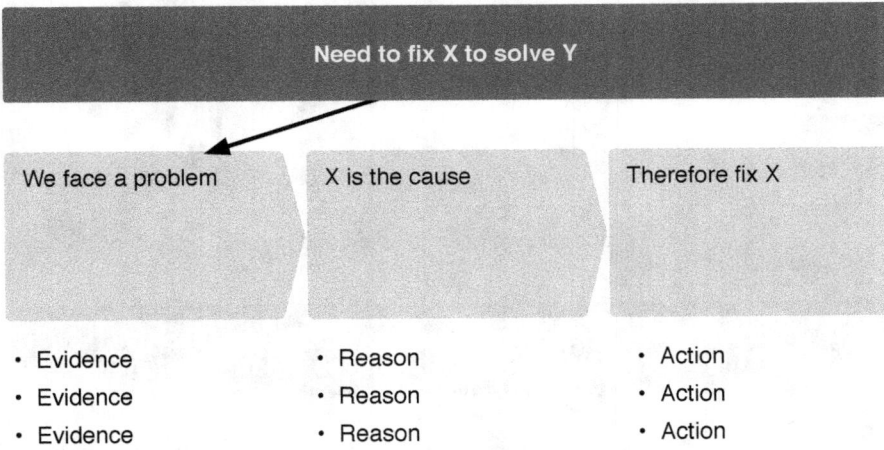

Need to fix X to solve Y		
We face a problem	X is the cause	Therefore fix X

- Evidence
- Evidence
- Evidence

- Reason
- Reason
- Reason

- Action
- Action
- Action

Use Houston when you must convince an audience of a problem and talk them through actions

Like any deductive storyline, Houston takes the audience through a set of premises that result in one clear recommendation. It's great for convincing audiences that may be sceptical, or when you only have one opportunity to present both the problem and your recommendations. This might occur with a board or governance committee when you want to provide an update *and* drive to action in the one meeting. Here are two examples.

Example: explaining a performance gap

Houston, We Have a Problem helped a finance team we worked with explain a performance gap to a business unit leadership team and outline a set of actions. The storyline is on the following page.

BigBank storyline

Context	Each month Finance reviews BigBank financial performance to identify whether the business unit is on track to achieve its full year target and what actions are needed to improve performance
Trigger	February financials are now in
Question	What actions do we need to take based on February financials?

BigBank needs to close the projected M$X revenue shortfall by focusing on A and B under-performance during March

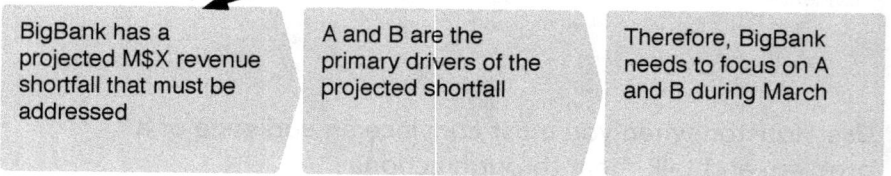

BigBank has a projected M$X revenue shortfall that must be addressed	A and B are the primary drivers of the projected shortfall	Therefore, BigBank needs to focus on A and B during March

• February results show a M$X revenue shortfall
 	
• Current trajectory indicates BigBank is forecast for a full year M$X revenue shortfall
	• Product A revenues are down M$X
	  – Volumes are down M$Y to target
	  – A margins are AAAbps below target
	• Product B are down M$X because of X and Y margin
	• Product C is on track to target but below system as at February
	• Product D volumes are below target by M$X
		• Bring forward initiatives in Product A to potentially deliver M$X
		• Implement initiatives to potentially deliver M$Y revenue uplift in product B
		• Understand what's required to grow ZZZZ at target in product C
		• Track progress of customer offer initiative in Product D – tracking uplift

You can see that the context and trigger remind the audience of what the communication is about – in this case a regular finance team update to the business unit leadership team. The core of the storyline outlines the performance issue, the looming shortfall and the major causes of that shortfall, as well as the steps required to fix it.

This storyline was used to define the architecture for a PowerPoint pack, which finance used to guide the conversation with the business unit leadership team.

As you can imagine, the pack was not a short one. Although the high-level ideas are simple, they were supported by extensive analysis that the leadership needed to work through. The team was prepared for a robust conversation as presentations about shortfalls and under-performance almost always lead to tough questions, if not a thorough grilling.

The team began their story by explaining the significance of the revenue shortfall, as without an understanding that this was pivotal to bank performance, there was no story to tell. Once there was agree-ment on this point, the team could then move on to explain what had caused the shortfall.

This again was a tough message to deliver as it painted a difficult picture for some product lines and the teams in charge of them. Those on the leadership team who had responsibility for these areas had been briefed in advance, and even though accepting of the reality and part of the solution described in the third section, they were never going to make the meeting an easy one.

The final leg of the story was easier to present as the bad news had been agreed upon, and everyone was primed for action to correct the problems they knew existed. Importantly, it covered what needed to happen in all four product areas, not just Products A and B, but the storyline does call for a focus on those underperforming products.

Example: a team briefing

Houston, We Have a Problem is a great storyline structure for the short, sharp team briefing. For example, if a team member wanted to update a project leader on what needed to happen to ensure a piece of analytical work was completed, she might use Houston.

On the following page is an example based on a Houston storyline a client used recently. Given the meeting was informal and short, she used a hand-written sketch of the storyline. Jotting the ideas down helped her collect her thoughts, and the visual structure helped to keep her on point and made it easy to reference.

Marketing model storyline

Context	As you know I'm building the model we'll use to predict sales volumes
Trigger	We need to have it completed by Friday to run the model in time for the meeting on Tuesday
Question	How are we tracking?

We need Marketing to provide the latest sales data to finish the model

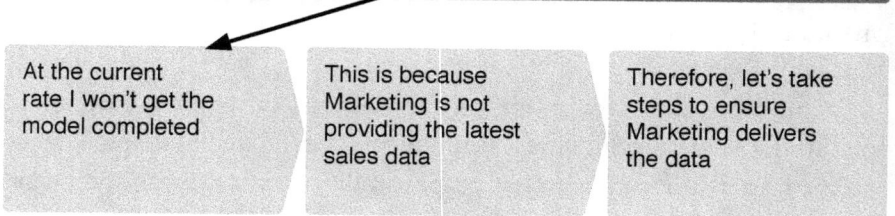

At the current rate I won't get the model completed	This is because Marketing is not providing the latest sales data	Therefore, let's take steps to ensure Marketing delivers the data
• We've put in a series of data requests that we said we needed to get by early Friday • We've got an incomplete data set • We're running out of time to test the model	• Marketing has the latest sales data • The Marketing Analyst is not giving us the data as he does not see it as a priority	• Call the Head of Marketing to hurry things up with the analyst • Check in again 9 am Friday • Run the model as planned before our meeting on Tuesday

Understand that Houston maps problems, the cause and resulting steps

Houston outlines the case for action based on a specific cause or set of causes. There are some key elements you must get right if you want to be convincing:

• *The 'So what' must be a recommendation which also includes the reason why it is the **right** recommendation.* In the example above, it is, 'We need Marketing to provide the latest sales data to finish the model'. This sentence explains *what* we need to happen (get Marketing to provide the latest sales data) and *why* (to finish the model). Either of those points on its own is not sufficient for the 'So what' in a Houston story.

- The statement and comment must of course lead to actions – they should remind the audience about what has been agreed, and lead to a 'how' question. But, be careful to test that the audience really does need a Houston storyline and does need convincing about why action is needed or why certain steps are required. If they only need a 'why' story, The Pitch might be a better alternative (discussed on page 59).

- The statement must highlight that the issue is serious – or at least serious enough to warrant attention. The comment identifies the cause (or sometimes causes) of that problem. It must make the case that this is (or these are) the cause of the problem. Then the recommendation is supported by actions. Be careful to ensure that the actions address the cause or causes outlined in the comment.

Avoid overkill; Houston is about convincing

There are three traps to avoid when using Houston:

1 This storyline is about convincing – don't use it if the audience already knows about the problem and its cause. If they do, taking them through all that again can be boring and frustrating. As a client once said to us when complaining about the information developed by a consulting team, 'Don't waste time telling me what I already know!'

2 Equally, be careful to avoid this pattern if your audience is the cause of the problem! There are usually many ways to tell a story, and inflaming or embarrassing stakeholders is unlikely to help your cause.

3 The other trap is an obvious one: as with all deductive storylines, the problem and the cause must be linked correctly. For Houston to work as a storyline the cause must be 'the' cause or set of causes. If it's just 'a' cause then the 'therefore' does not follow as the only sensible path to take to solve the core problem you are discussing.

TO B OR NOT TO B – FOR EXPLAINING WHICH OPTION IS BEST

Did Hamlet realise he was describing one of the classic business story-lines when he uttered those immortal words, 'to be or not to be'? Well, probably not. But, in business we are often asked to assess options and make a recommendation.

Too often we see leaders asserting that everyone should follow the option they are recommending, without explaining *why* it's the right option. They just say 'follow me', which is often ineffective if the audience doesn't have anything else to go on.

Instead, our classic storyline pattern – To B or Not to B – takes the audience on the journey through the thinking that makes the case for your preferred option.

To make this pattern work for you, you must:

- know that To B or Not to B argues for one particular option

- use To B or Not to B to take your audience on the journey through your thinking

- understand that To B or Not to B enables you to explain first, recommend last

- make sure it's complete – this story is great when you need to work through all the options, not just one option that you like.

Let's consider each of these.

Understand that To B or Not to B argues for one particular option

To B or Not to B is a simple 'options' story that we see used often. It's great for explaining a problem to an audience, taking them through the options (A, B and C), explaining why your preferred option (B) is best, and what needs to happen to implement your preferred option.

To B or Not to B pattern

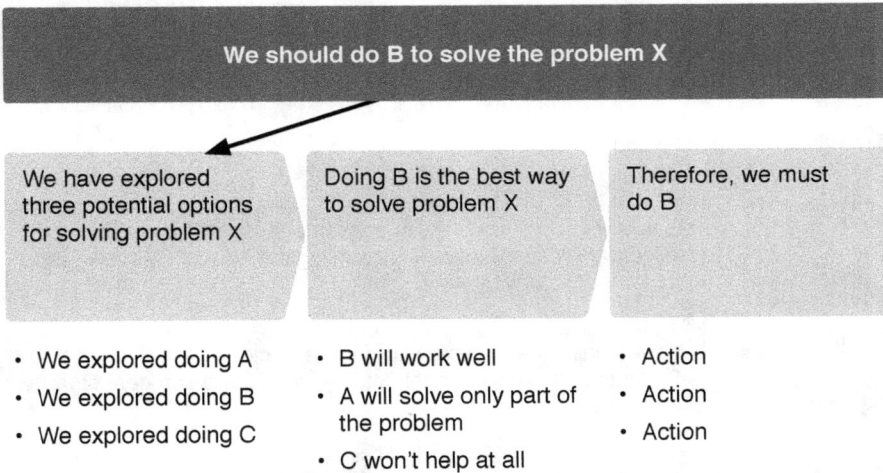

We should do B to solve the problem X

We have explored three potential options for solving problem X	Doing B is the best way to solve problem X	Therefore, we must do B

• We explored doing A • We explored doing B • We explored doing C	• B will work well • A will solve only part of the problem • C won't help at all	• Action • Action • Action

Use To B or Not to B to take your audience on the journey through your thinking

Choose the To B or Not to B storyline when you need to educate your audience about *why* action is needed, *what options* are on the table, and the *action plan* they will need to implement. This might be when you need to present a paper to a senior team or a board when they need to understand what needs to be done and why. Equally, it might help engage your team when they need to put your recommendation into action.

Like all our storyline patterns, we see this being useful in multiple situations.

Example: the business case

This is powerful when recommending a course of action. To B or Not to B is a great business case structure when you must convince your audience of the best option and a course of action in just one conversation. An IT team used this storyline pattern to convince the Chief Operating Officer (COO) to invest in a technology service provider's solution to a data management problem. The storyline had to be tight and clear: the IT team had failed to win support for other projects as they had confused the COO with too much technical detail.

Here's how they used To B or Not to B to engage the COO this time, using the storyline to frame the architecture of a PowerPoint pack.

Coonawarra Corp storyline

Context	As you will recall from recent conversations, effective cloud-based data management is increasingly critical to Coonawarra Corp's technology strategy
Trigger	We've undertaken a review to help us decide how to manage key elements of one component: intelligent cloud-based data storage capabilities
Question	How should we manage intelligent cloud-based data storage?

Coonawarra Corp should invest $300K–$400K in Black to ensure it has intelligent cloud-based data storage capabilities

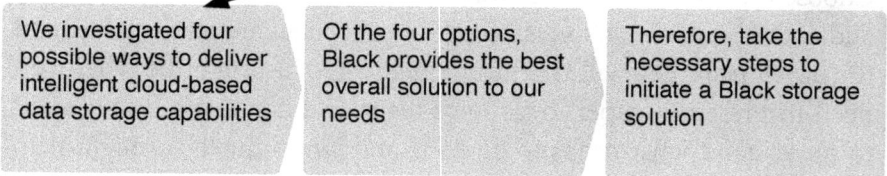

We investigated four possible ways to deliver intelligent cloud-based data storage capabilities	Of the four options, Black provides the best overall solution to our needs	Therefore, take the necessary steps to initiate a Black storage solution
A We investigated outsourcing to Yellow as competitor A has done so	• Black meets all key requirements	• Allocate $300K–$400K
B We investigated working with Black given our historic relationship	• Yellow meets many of the basic requirements but lacks industry maturity	• Agree partnering arrangements with Black
C We considered Pink given competitor B has used Pink's technology successfully	• Pink could meet the basic requirements as a retrofit to current storage but adoption of their technology introduces unneeded complexity	• Develop a data migration plan
D We considered insourcing given the IT team is excited by the challenge and it would broaden their capabilities	• Managing it internally is not possible as we lack the skills	• Develop a risk management plan

You can see that there is a 'given' established in the CTQ that needed no justification or explanation with the COO: intelligent cloud-based data management is critical. Also, the team wanted to let the COO know they had been digging into the issue. Their recommendation was clear: go with 'Black'.

The underpinning logic of the storyline enabled the team to take the COO on the journey quickly:

- The first statement described the options that the team had analysed: there were three potential organisations they could engage going forward – 'Black', 'Yellow' and 'Pink' – and they needed to describe each one at the start.

- The second section evaluated the options: it was important to put up *all* the options to be considered. Each option was analysed against the same criteria – cost, budget, technical solution offered, and so on – and 'Black' emerged as a clear winner.

- The final section outlined the action plan at a high level, and was only discussed once the COO was on board with the idea that there was a problem to solve and that going with Black was the right way to do it.

The result? They got the decision they wanted, and the COO told the team that if they presented business cases like that in the future he'd approve everything – fast!

Example: outsource or insource?
To B or Not to B is powerful when explaining what courses of action someone should take when confronted with an underperforming vendor.

In this example a manager was concerned about the performance of a vendor and wanted to recommend bringing the service in house. He developed a simple To B or Not to B storyline and presented it in a Steering Committee meeting.

The storyline is deceptively simple and high level, and was used to guide the conversation. The manager rightly expected to be grilled on the details and to receive thorough and specific questions about the problems with the ServCo arrangement and the risks of bringing the project in house.

One of the Steering Committee members had their reputation at stake given they had recommended going with ServCo. Even though the team had kept this person across the problems as they emerged, this person had some tough questions. However, the team was ready, and provided enough evidence that the leadership as a whole agreed the service should be brought in house.

Here's the storyline they used.

Bondi Compliance storyline

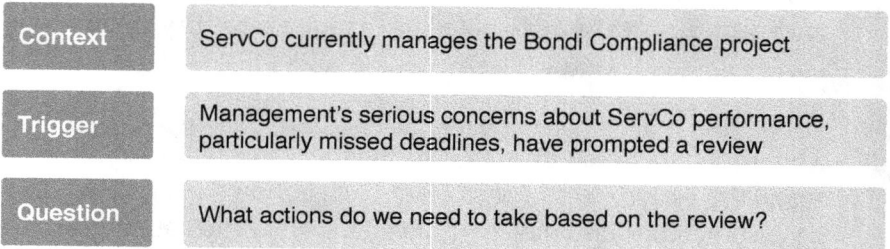

Context	ServCo currently manages the Bondi Compliance project
Trigger	Management's serious concerns about ServCo performance, particularly missed deadlines, have prompted a review
Question	What actions do we need to take based on the review?

We recommend terminating the ServCo arrangement, bringing the Bondi Compliance work in house to ensure the project delivers on its objectives

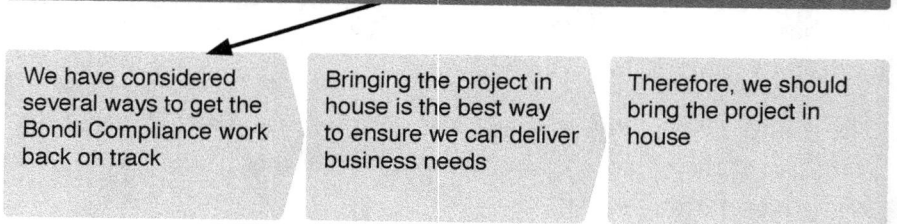

We have considered several ways to get the Bondi Compliance work back on track	Bringing the project in house is the best way to ensure we can deliver business needs	Therefore, we should bring the project in house
A We have considered placing ServCo on hold and bringing them back later B We have considered bringing the compliance work completely in house C We have considered implementing a tactical solution using spreadsheets	• Placing ServCo on hold and bringing back later is possible but unattractive as it maintains the relationship but the costs would be massive • Bringing the compliance work in house is cost-effective and will deliver desired outcomes • Implementing a tactical solution of using spreadsheets is simple but the risks are major	• Terminate the ServCo arrangement • Reconfirm the project requirements • Refine deadlines to catch up in relation to deadlines • Complete solution development

Understand that To B or Not to B enables you to explain first, recommend last

So, how does it work? To B or Not to B maps options, and recommends a course of action. There are some key elements you must get right:

- *The introduction must set up the story that's coming.* But, be careful not to introduce material that will require justification – that should be in the main part of the storyline, not in the introduction.

- *The 'So what' must be a recommendation that also explains why your solution should be adopted.* In this type of story the 'So what' synthesises the whole story, but – as in all deductive storylines – rests heavily on the 'therefore' point. That is, after all, the point of the story – is it B or not B? Make sure you don't fall into the trap of just stating, 'There are three options'.

- *The logic must work.* The 'statement' must outline the options available. The 'comment' lays out the reasons why one of the options – B – is best, which leads to the 'therefore' point, which explains to the audience what steps are required. The key is to ensure – as with all deductive storylines – that the statement and comment are 'true', and that the comment really does comment on the statement.

- *It needs to be right for your audience.* To B or Not to B works well when you have only one shot at communicating with your audience and you need to take them on the journey. Only use it if they don't already know the details surrounding the problem. Otherwise you'll just annoy them telling them things they already know.

Make sure the options are complete

There is an obvious trap to avoid here. The problem and options must be linked, with the problem also being serious enough to warrant action. The audience must agree with you that the problem is worth solving before you take them to the next phase, where you explain the options you see for solving that problem.

You must also present a complete, mutually exclusive set of options. That's where the audience's mind will go once they agree that there's a problem worth solving.

In the example described above the problem could be dealt with internally or with outside assistance. So, it was critical that both options were analysed thoroughly or the audience would not necessarily agree that bringing the project in house was the best option.

WATCH OUT – TO COUNTER EMERGING RISKS

We've all heard it before: 'Yes, that's okay, *but* … ' Well, this is the basis of one of our classic business storylines. We call it Watch Out for a reason: it's a warning storyline that tells your audience there are risks ahead that must be managed. Like Houston, it's not just about the warning, it drives the audience to the steps required to address the risks ahead.

To make this pattern work for you, you must:

- know that Watch Out combines what's working, risks and action in the same story
- use Watch Out to persuade your audience on the need to change direction
- know that Watch Out maps what's succeeded, the risks and their remedies
- avoid crafting a narrative that flows without compelling logic.

Let's discuss each of these.

Understand that Watch Out combines what's working, risks and action in the same story

Watch Out is a simple deductive storyline. It makes the argument that action is required to address risks that are important enough to warrant attention.

Watch Out pattern

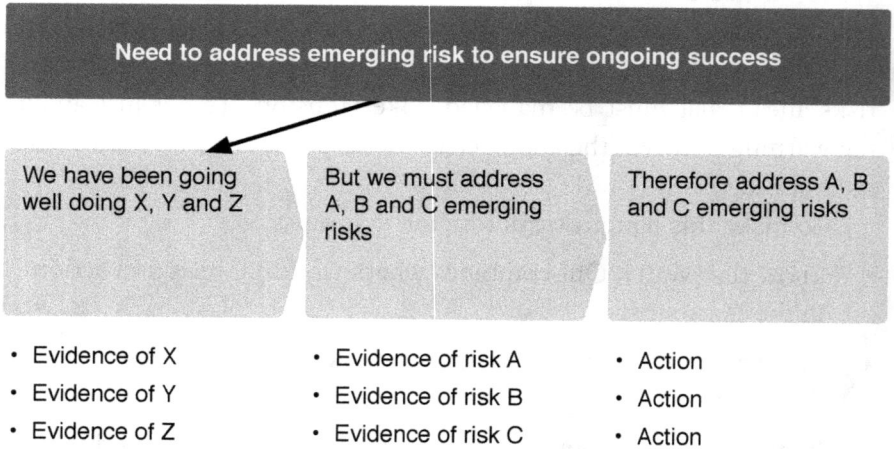

Need to address emerging risk to ensure ongoing success		
We have been going well doing X, Y and Z	But we must address A, B and C emerging risks	Therefore address A, B and C emerging risks
• Evidence of X • Evidence of Y • Evidence of Z	• Evidence of risk A • Evidence of risk B • Evidence of risk C	• Action • Action • Action

Use Watch Out to persuade your audience on the need to change direction

Like any deductive storyline, Watch Out takes the audience through a set of premises that results in one clear recommendation – the 'therefore'. It's great for convincing audiences that action is required or where you only have one opportunity to communicate with the decision makers – such as with a board or governance committee where you want to provide an update *and* drive to action. The difference with this storyline is that it's all about risks and managing them.

Example: the 'uh-oh' moment

Watch Out helped a project leader make the case for action with a Steering Committee. Here's the storyline.

The BigCo Risks storyline

Context	Project Big is a collaborative project between BigCo and TechCo for putting administrative services in the cloud – it will transform administrative service delivery
Trigger	The Project has faced severe problems in delivering to its agreed timelines
Question	What should the Project Big Steering Committee focus on now to ensure successful delivery?

We need your support to give us the time and flexibility over the next 2 weeks to manage emerging risks that are threatening timelines

We have now demonstrated clearly that the integrated BigCo–TechCo solution works	However, we now face risks that threaten our go-to-market timelines	Therefore, we need time to manage critical project risks
• Proven that we can do A • Proven that we can do B • Proven that we can do C	• Design delayed due to X • Inadequate skill sets and unclear responsibilities are impacting on technology solution design • Delays in security sign-off are threatening our ability to support products	• Signal a likely delay in delivering technology • Allow the team 2 weeks to undertake discovery and report back with an impact assessment of technology delay • Arrange meetings with security to develop risk management strategy

This was just one of many projects reporting that day. As a result, the context and trigger remind the Steering Committee of what the project is about and the issues they looked at last time. Importantly, the question is all about what the Steering Committee must do. The 'So what' for the storyline highlights the actions that the project leader wants the Steering Committee to take.

The supporting logic is deductive, as we've said. It outlines the big wins the project has had in the 'statement'. Importantly, in the 'comment' the point is made that risks are emerging that *must* be addressed. Without this imperative, these might be any old risks. Then the 'therefore' follows – let's address those risks.

Watch Out, like many others, is also a great storyline structure for the short, sharp team briefing.

Example: the leadership team 'heads up' update
Watch Out helped a team member provide a 'heads up' update for the leadership team. Typically, she would have used a pack of spreadsheets to provide a numbers-based update. Instead, she took what was for her a big risk – she spoke about the update, using the storyline to guide the conversation.

The storyline is on the following page.

Here are some subtleties to note about this storyline that made it work:

- The context and trigger reminded the leadership gently about the objectives of the strategy – they have bold aspirations.

- Importantly, the question is focused on 'action', not just an update.

- The structure of the storyline was also important. The deductive structure allowed her to tell them about FY17 wins, drill into the FY18 concerns (that were definitely serious enough to warrant action), and then focus on some key actions that she wanted to recommend (gently) to the leadership team.

Once she finished her update she received a round of applause from the leadership team!

The Heads Up storyline

Context — Our new strategy – Fruit Growth – was designed to give us a big lift in performance and you have asked Finance to review our performance to date

Trigger — We reviewed results to the end of Feb. with a view to deciding on what actions are needed to deliver against our industry strategy

Question — What actions are needed?

We need to work together to deliver more consistent results that demonstrate we are on the right track to deliver against our industry strategy

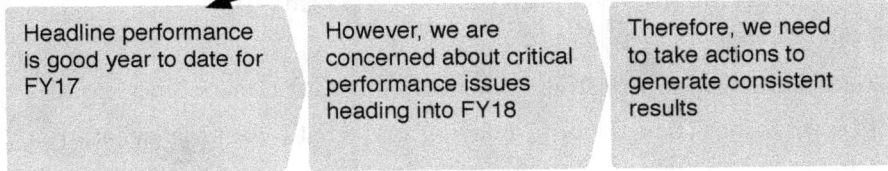

Headline performance is good year to date for FY17	However, we are concerned about critical performance issues heading into FY18	Therefore, we need to take actions to generate consistent results
• Total fruit revenues for FY17 are on or above target across all target categories • All key target segments are on or above track to achieve KPI targets for FY17: – Managed margins well – Good mix in the growth	• Fruit revenue growth is patchy across categories: – Good growth in Bananas, Apples and Oranges – Below expectations in Pears, Nectarines and Cherries • Customer NPS is patchy: – Bananas performing strongly – Stone fruits are not increasing in popularity	1 Continue strong margin management across all segments 2 Conduct deep dive by segment on growth potential 3 Understand poor NPS drivers in Bananas and Stone Fruit

Understand that Watch Out maps what's succeeded, the risks and the remedies

There are some key elements of the storyline you must get right:

- *The CTQ must lead to a question about action* (as with the questions in all deductive storylines).

- *The 'So what' must be a recommendation for action that also includes why that recommendation is the right one.* It may be a recommendation such as: 'We should do X to achieve Y.'

- *Each major part of the storyline must do its job* – in this example the 'statement' describes what's been working, the 'comment' describes the risks that must be managed for the overall task to be a success, and the 'therefore' point outlines the actions required to address the risks and keep the project on track.

Avoid crafting a narrative that flows without compelling logic

Don't fall into the trap of just laying out what's working, what's not, and actions. A flow of ideas that simply relate to the same topic is not sufficiently compelling to encourage your audience to agree with the actions recommended. The logic must compel the audience to act on your specific recommendation.

The comment is key. In the earlier Project Big example it was clear that if the risks were not managed then the go-to-market timetable would not be met, which was a completely unacceptable outcome. So, action was *necessary*, not just 'nice to have'.

* * * * *

So, now you've seen seven of our classic storyline patterns. Now we want to shift gear – to look at how you use a storyline to shape the communication you share.

CHAPTER FOUR

USING STORYLINES TO SHAPE THE COMMUNICATION YOU DELIVER

Now that you understand how to structure a storyline either from scratch or using a pattern, let's now consider how to convert your storyline into a piece of clear and compelling communication.

There are steps to take to prepare your material, and this also provides opportunities to revisit your ideas about purpose and audience to ensure your content is both logical *and* engaging. There are also opportunities to think carefully about other aspects of stakeholder management that are critical to getting your proposition across.

Design, Develop, Deliver framework

Deliver communication

- Package it (email, prose, pack, etc.)
- Communicate it (clearly, powerfully)
- Get feedback (so you can continuously improve)

Design strategy

- Purpose: I want my audience to …
- Audience: decision makers, influencers, others …
- Medium: pack, paper, email, verbal, meeting, other?
- Process: sign offs, delivery deadlines

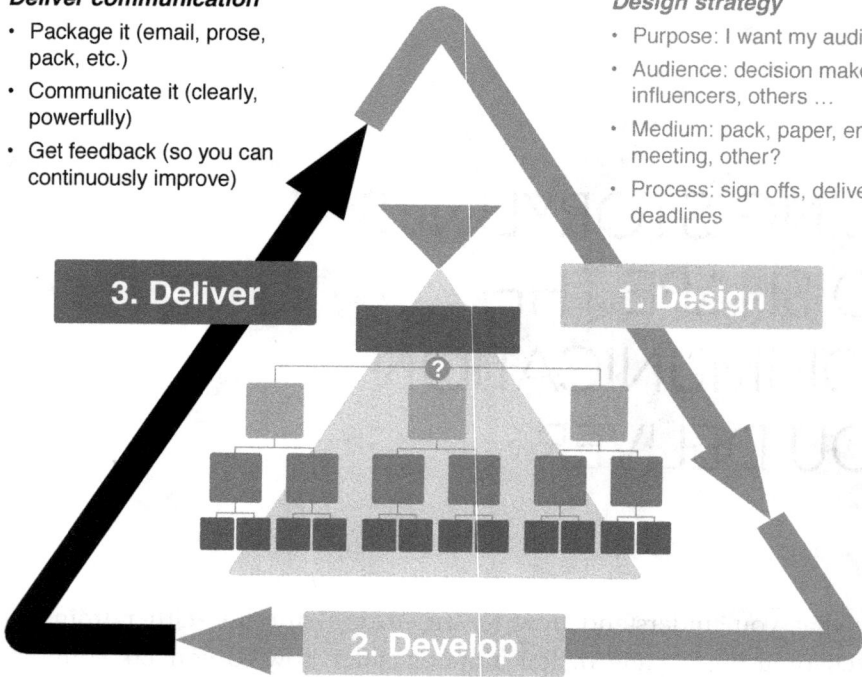

3. Deliver

1. Design

2. Develop

Develop storyline (with a pattern or without)

- Clarify introduction (context, trigger, question)
- Articulate 'So what' (powerful, less than 25 words)
- Map out logical support (grouping or deductive)
- Test the storyline (with 10-Point Test, peers and stakeholders)

We're now up to step three of the Design, Develop, Deliver approach. When converting your storyline into a piece of communication that enables you to share your ideas, we encourage you to do three things:

- package your ideas into the most useful medium for this communication (for example, an email, a report, a PowerPoint pack, a speech, or potentially something more creative)

- communicate your ideas clearly and powerfully

- get feedback so you can continuously improve.

Let's now discuss each of these in more detail.

Now it's time to get soft!

It may sound unusual to think about communication in mechanical terms that revolve around thinking, logic and rules. You may worry that this removes the need to accommodate the 'softer' aspects of communication.

The storyline structure requires you to think carefully about your audience's needs in relation to the content. Once that is done, it's time to think carefully about how to share your communication with your audience for maximum impact. In this phase you will consider the softer elements, such as language, tone, delivery style, and whether to include personal anecdotes or metaphors to reinforce a point that may be hard to explain.

PACKAGING YOUR IDEAS INTO THE MOST USEFUL MEDIUM

One of the positive outcomes of using storylines to organise your thinking before you communicate is that once the storyline is ready, so is your thinking. You then need to choose the best medium to communicate this story. The communication itself can take a variety of forms, including:

- an email

- a formal speech

- a paper
- a presentation pack
- a verbal briefing
- a workshop.

Or it could be something completely different and creative – it doesn't matter. The options and combinations are endless. The key is to ensure the medium you choose makes it easy for the audience to follow your storyline.

Your chosen form of communication should help to portray the meaning of the communication. So, even though the packaging differs, there are still some important guidelines for the most common types of communication – emails, papers, presentations and verbal updates. You should:

- **Include an introduction** so the communication can be understood by someone who is 'not in the room'. The only time this doesn't really apply is if you are in the middle of an email exchange where the context is known. The question in your CTQ guides the shape of your introduction and communication, but you do not necessarily need to include it.

- **Talk through the 'So what' and top level of the story** up front. Taken together with the context and trigger, this makes for a great summary for busy executives. Doing this is a game changer – it puts you in charge of the story while also enabling the audience to quickly decide what they want to know more about. Some of our clients use the storyline page to do this. It's up to you and what works with your audiences.

- **Use the format of your communication to help signpost the storyline**.

    In a *presentation pack*, this means you can include 'tracker' pages so the audience knows where they are up to, and possibly mini versions of the tracker image in the top right corner of each page in longer packs.

    In a *prose-style paper*, this means combining messages with visual cues – such as font style and size – to help the audience know how important an idea is within the context of the whole story. Using key messages as titles or headings also makes it easier for the audience to skim the document to find the sections that interest them most.

If it's a simple *5- to 10-line email*, you might dot point the key ideas or highlight them in bold.

The Coonawarra Corp example in appendix A illustrates one way of using a storyline within a prose-style document.

- **Use visuals** well in both prose-style papers and PowerPoint. Visuals are a great way to cut verbiage and highlight your key points – so long as they are used well. The trick is to work out your message first, and then ensure your visuals support or add to that message and do not distract the audience.*

- **Don't be afraid of PowerPoint**, but make sure you use it well. One of the corporate world's biggest gripes is PowerPoint. Some executives have even banned it. But we don't think PowerPoint is the problem – it's how it's used. If a PowerPoint pack is well structured with a clear storyline, it can be a great communication tool. (We've provided an annotated example of a PowerPoint pack in appendix B to show you how a storyline connects with actual pieces of communication.)

Although storylines provide the best architecture for business communication, we realise that at times you may have to work within the confines of templates. Many of these accommodate storylines easily, allowing for the storyline to be incorporated into the relevant areas of the template. Alternatively, the storyline can become an add-on to a data pack which drives the conversations about the insights gleaned from the data. Either way, the key is to ensure you can organise your ideas logically so you can present a clear point of view.

Once you have made these decisions about the format of your communication, you can easily prepare your communication and be ready to deliver it.

---

* Gene Zelazny's book *Say it with Charts* provides two very useful frameworks for thinking about visuals that represent concepts and visuals that represent data.

DELIVERING YOUR IDEAS CLEARLY AND POWERFULLY

There are shelves and shelves of books and thousands and thousands of web pages devoted to the art of communication, so we won't replicate that here. When it comes to communicating a business storyline, however, four things are essential:

- Confirm your stakeholder management strategy.
- Practise your delivery and your Q&A.
- Communicate your storyline sequentially.
- Be open to the idea that a one-page storyline may be enough on its own.

Let's now discuss each of these.

Confirm your stakeholder management strategy

Firstly, confirm your stakeholder management strategy. Few audiences – whether they are senior, peer or junior – are uncritical or devoid of their own agendas.

At the start of the book we considered the importance of being clear about your purpose and understanding your audience deeply. Now is the time to revisit those two things and confirm that you have an effective stakeholder management strategy[*] in place before you deliver your communication.

Where high-stakes communication is concerned, you will most likely have been talking with key stakeholders or their representatives about contentious issues in parallel with preparing the final communication. You will hopefully have talked with them about the high-level storyline as a whole to test whether it covers the necessary issues and provides a 'So what' that makes sense from their perspective.

You should also be listening carefully to learn more about their agenda and any politics around the issues. This will help you flush out questions you might be asked, identify where you need to drill down, and decide how to address the tougher challenges that may be raised.

---

[*] See the Clarity College Resources section near the end of this book for a pointer towards a short article and a video on this subject.

If a communication is less sensitive, it's still worth checking with your peers at a minimum to test the storyline and check whether you have missed anything. A fresh set of eyes at this point cannot be under-estimated, even when a story is logically strong. It must be strong both in terms of its structure and its content, and sometimes it takes an objective outsider to identify where the content is flawed – or at the most basic level where there are typos or grammatical errors that could be embarrassing.

Storylines in both theory and practice

The lengths people go to during this stakeholder engagement process can be intriguing.

One senior banker routinely spends quite some time during the day that his more critical board papers are due to-ing and fro-ing with the company secretary to confirm where his presen-tation would fall in the order of the board meeting, who would be presenting before and after him, and on what topic.

Although he rarely adjusts the substance of his storyline, he does adjust certain details to reflect his 'batting order'. If, for example, he discovered that he was presenting after a highly technical and detailed topic, he would consciously double check that his explanations were easy to follow.

If he was following someone else who was also asking for a large amount of money for a project, he would factor this into the way he began his own pitch – particularly if he was also asking for a sizable sum.

He also took advice from the company secretary on points that might go in or be removed to increase his chance of success.

This example reminds us how complex the stakeholder man-agement process can be, and – although we are of course a little biased – how useful storylines can be to help us make conscious and deliberate choices about how to deliver engaging messages without detracting from the substance of our recommendations.

Practise your communication

We encourage our clients to find a way to practise when they are presenting to a group of people.

If you are confident in your content and comfortable that your audience will be more interested than challenging, practising may involve locking yourself away for a short time to read the story through to imagine yourself giving the presentation. Standard team meetings or huddles might be an example of this, or potentially routine updates to a Steering Committee or leadership team.

However, if you expect a more challenging audience, we recommend rehearsing in front of your colleagues who can role play the more challenging characters you will face. They can throw questions at you, interrupt you, and attempt to throw you off your game to strengthen your responses and your confidence.

In short, the higher the stakes for the presentation, the more effort we encourage you to invest in this rehearsal process. It is central to smoothing out any wrinkles and building confidence. And, it can also highlight where your storyline needs to be strengthened or changed.

Communicate your storyline sequentially

The third consideration, in the vast majority of cases, is to communicate your storyline sequentially. Again this varies based on the audience, your objectives and your data. Typically though, there is an order to the communication of a storyline that matches the order in which you think the ideas need to be delivered.

Opposite is a snapshot of how we encourage our clients to do this, using a one-page storyline as the reference point. The same principles apply if you are using a prose-style paper or a PowerPoint pack to guide your conversation: start at the beginning and work your way through the story step by step.

Be open to the idea that a one-page storyline may be enough

Lastly, it helps to be open to the idea that the one-page storyline may be enough on its own, or perhaps supported by a couple of data pages. Even if you initially think you need to prepare a 12- or 15-page data pack, once you have developed your storyline you may find that the one-pager is enough.

Communicating a typical storyline

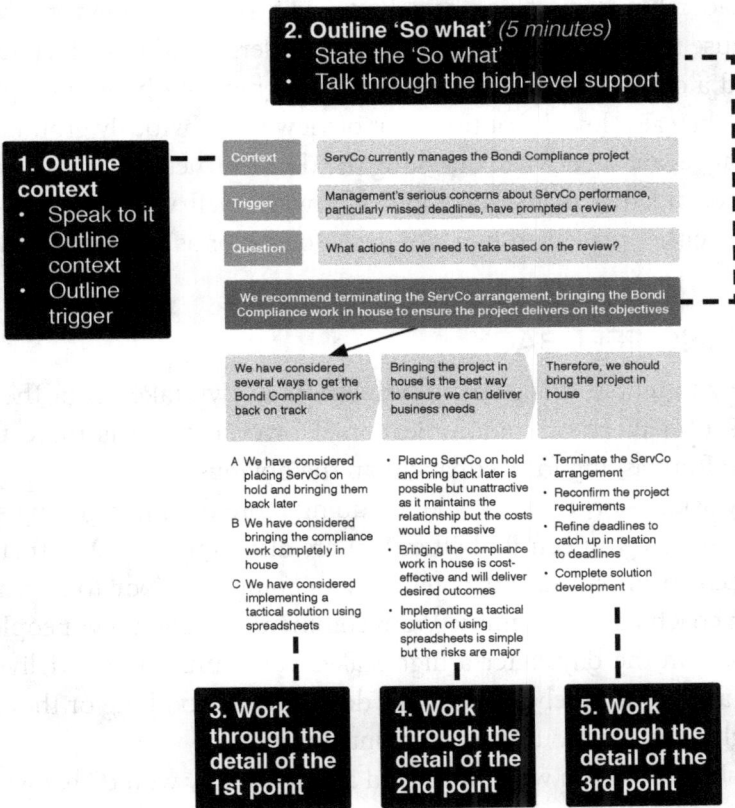

2. Outline 'So what' *(5 minutes)*
- State the 'So what'
- Talk through the high-level support

1. Outline context
- Speak to it
- Outline context
- Outline trigger

Context	ServCo currently manages the Bondi Compliance project
Trigger	Management's serious concerns about ServCo performance, particularly missed deadlines, have prompted a review
Question	What actions do we need to take based on the review?

We recommend terminating the ServCo arrangement, bringing the Bondi Compliance work in house to ensure the project delivers on its objectives

| We have considered several ways to get the Bondi Compliance work back on track | Bringing the project in house is the best way to ensure we can deliver business needs | Therefore, we should bring the project in house |

A We have considered placing ServCo on hold and bringing them back later	• Placing ServCo on hold and bring back later is possible but unattractive as it maintains the relationship but the costs would be massive	• Terminate the ServCo arrangement
B We have considered bringing the compliance work completely in house	• Bringing the compliance work in house is cost-effective and will deliver desired outcomes	• Reconfirm the project requirements
C We have considered implementing a tactical solution using spreadsheets	• Implementing a tactical solution of using spreadsheets is simple but the risks are major	• Refine deadlines to catch up in relation to deadlines • Complete solution development

3. Work through the detail of the 1st point

4. Work through the detail of the 2nd point

5. Work through the detail of the 3rd point

In fact, some boards and leadership teams of large Australian companies are now using one-page storylines as the focal point of their discussions. The one-pager is often supported by a small number of charts that are only brought out to answer questions.

In an example of this, just recently one of our clients chose to present a one-page storyline to an executive team rather than data in spreadsheets. She projected a one-page storyline like the one above on a screen and worked through it progressively. First, she discussed the context and trigger. She then clicked on the 'So what', then the top line, and then each set of supporting points, finishing with the action. It only took five minutes, and the leadership team knew exactly where the finance team thought the business should focus.

The result – after explaining that she was trying something different and then diving into her update – was a round of applause from the leadership team. This was definitely a first. She had never received applause for a presentation before. The leaders loved that she had presented a clear point of view without going blow by blow through the data. They also loved that the point of view was obviously grounded in substance, and that when checking the data the messaging stacked up.

We find that many stakeholders engage well with the high-level outline either presented in a 'dot dash' format or as a visual storyline.

GETTING FEEDBACK

It's easy to ignore this step and rely on your own take about the outcomes of a piece of communication. However, there is more to be gained from asking for feedback than the obvious.

By asking for feedback you are doing more than just getting some ideas on how you can do better. You are also demonstrating that you are keen to improve, and potentially opening the door to a mentoring or coaching opportunity. We recommend asking a few people for feedback in the days after a high-stakes communication is delivered. Don't ask immediately, but equally don't leave it too long or they may struggle to recall enough useful points for you.

Ask each person what they liked and what they would change, and don't be afraid to probe. Ask them what they liked about your presentation style, the way you handled questions, and the logic of your storyline. Ask them if they liked the visuals you used, and whether there were enough or too many.

Also, don't be afraid to ask them what they remember about your key messages to see if they were powerful enough to 'stick' in their minds. This is particularly important if you have presented to a leadership team, Steering Committee or board, as they will probably have sat through many presentations the day you presented. You need your messages to 'stick' well enough that you and your recommendations stand out for the right reasons.

This doesn't have to be formal, but it should be a part of your process.

FIVE

INTRODUCING STORYLINING IN YOUR BUSINESS

As we have worked with more and more teams, and the leaders of those teams have been promoted, we have found ourselves working with increasingly larger teams. This has led us to develop ways to help large groups – and whole organisations – put these ideas into practice.

Whether you are an individual wanting to use storylines, a small team or a larger business wanting to implement the approach, the principles are simple, but it does take commitment and discipline. It is about changing behaviours.

These are our five key actions that leaders can take to put story-lining into practice in their business:

- Be clear about your purpose and expectations.[*]

- Put simple support systems and structures in place to drive changes in behaviour.

- Allow time to master the fundamental skills.

---

[*]   We have drawn on a change management framework described in *The McKinsey Quarterly*, 'The Psychology of Change Management', 2003 Special Edition.

- Find and encourage role models.
- Plan to make it stick.

Let's talk about each of these actions in some detail.

BEING CLEAR ABOUT YOUR PURPOSE AND EXPECTATIONS

If you want your team to adopt the storylining approach, be sure to explain specifically why it matters to you, why you think it should matter to them, and where mastering storylining should fit in their priorities.

A Head of Finance recently made the case strongly: *you must be able to build and articulate a case (storyline) if you are to move beyond being a number cruncher to being a trusted adviser in the business*. He referred to examples in his staff who had done just that and were now in senior Finance roles with a seat at the leadership table.

But just talking about the 'why' is not enough. Leaders also must set the standards. There should be some simple expectations: that *everyone* must be good at storylining, and that *every document* – no matter how simple or complex – must be well targeted and well structured.

PUTTING SIMPLE SUPPORT SYSTEMS AND STRUCTURES IN PLACE

It's important that leaders put systems in place to support and encourage people to use storylining. Again the maxim is *keep it simple*. Leaders who are seeing great results put some simple measures in place. They:

- **Create a benchmark.** Leaders use the 10-Point Storyline Test (see chapter 2) to measure improvements in documents. This measures clarity, not just readability, which is important but not enough on its own. We see plenty of documents that seem well written that are not useful to the business.

- **Embed storylining in team and then individual performance indicators.** They set expectations that teams produce quality storylines and translate those into quality communication. Usually it makes sense to start with the team as a whole before focusing on individual performance indicators.

- **Build storylining into the operating rhythm.** Everyone is busy. Leaders understand that storylining requires an investment of time to get good results, and that investment needs to be part of 'the way we do things around here' and not just ad hoc. For teams that have regular outputs – for example, a monthly leadership briefing – they are scheduling a storylining meeting, for example, five days out from the briefing. Once they know the storyline, they can then develop a useful briefing package much more efficiently and with great time savings overall.

- **Make peer review part of the way things are done.** We cannot overstate the value of encouraging your team members to clarify their thinking on a single page before they prepare their final piece of communication. Oftentimes team members will have prepared a large amount of analysis in the form of spreadsheets and PowerPoint packs before they get to the storylining task. Do not allow them to use these as the starting point for their communication. Ask them to build a storyline and measure it against the 10-Point Storyline Test to provide constructive feedback before they build their pack.

ALLOWING TIME TO MASTER THE FUNDAMENTAL SKILLS

Becoming good at storylining – and delivering consistently powerful communication – requires practice, which takes time, which requires that practice be a priority. The 70–20–10 approach holds true: 70% of real learning happens on the job, 20% thanks to coaching, and 10% thanks to formal training sessions. Initial training sessions are important, but it's coaching and on-the-job learning that really matters.

Again, many successful leaders are implementing simple strategies that foster storyline learning. They include:

- coaching leaders in how to coach their teams in storylining using the Design, Develop, Deliver model and the 10-Point Storyline Test

- providing access to online or face-to-face learning for teams (if online, hold your team accountable for completing it!)

- scheduling storylining 'boot camp' sessions where teams come together for a few hours, share example storylines and peer review each other's work

- identifying people who have accountability for higher volumes of work or for higher priority communication and investing in one-on-one coaching for them by internal champions or external coaches.

FINDING AND ENCOURAGING ROLE MODELS

People need to see their leaders and peers using storylining if they are to be encouraged to do the same. If you take the approach seriously, so will your team. Again, there are some simple actions leaders can take to ensure their team members 'see' storylining in action:

- **Do it yourself.** Leaders must set the example – master the approach, storyline your communication, and ask people to be tough on you.

- **Incorporate storylining into your team meetings.** A team can discuss a relatively complex storyline in 5 to 10 minutes. Seeing examples helps everyone see patterns and get ideas. During the learning phase, team meetings can also be a great time to answer questions and challenge the team on their progress.

- **Build a library of good team storylining examples.** This is where patterns are powerful. Leaders can ask their teams to build up a library of team examples that others can follow.

- **Celebrate!** Some clients are holding Clarity 'best of' sessions where teams vote for the best examples by teams and individuals. Some are even channelling the Australian television awards, called the Logies, by calling them 'the Clarries'.

PLANNING TO MAKE IT STICK

Like any other business priority, leaders need to plan to make it happen. Leaders who take some simple steps to plan to make storylining stick will have a much greater chance of success. You can:

- **Identify clarity champions** in your teams who have the skills and desire to help drive a 'clarity plan'.

- **Build and sign off a plan** with the leadership team. Locking in a formal plan makes it real for teams and locks in leaders as well. The plan should cover how you will communicate, how you will develop skills in coaching and on-the-job leader and peer reviews, and what processes and system changes you will implement to foster changes in behaviour.

- **Work in 90-day 'sprints'.** Habits need to be formed fast, and we find the first 90 days are critical to building the skills in your teams. Initially the focus is on getting going with the creation of some great examples, some sessions to refresh learning, and the setting and delivery of team KPIs. At the end of the first 90 days, some leaders are sponsoring a 'Clarity Olympics' where teams and individuals submit storylines and get some feedback and recognition. It's all designed to create buzz around the idea.

- **Monitor progress.** It's as easy to miss incremental improvement as it is to let the approach slide as the team moves onto solving the next challenge. Here are 10 Key Indicators to watch for at the end of each sprint and at predetermined points afterwards.

10 KEY INDICATORS

What are you seeing *more* of?

1. The language of storylining being used in the office?
2. Colleagues thinking through storylines together while referring to the 10-point test?
3. Storylines being presented to you and other leaders (formally or informally) for review before papers and packs are prepared?
4. Communication that you and your peers can read and respond to quickly?
5. Positive feedback from audiences, such as senior leaders, customers and others?

What are you seeing *less* of?

6   Teams consistently working late to deliver routine papers?

7   Audiences asking clarification questions about your team's communication?

8   Leadership forums rejecting papers that contain good ideas?

9   Leadership forums receiving unnecessarily lengthy communication?

10 Fire-fighting stemming from poor communication?

NEXT STEPS FOR YOU

Having read this far you now know that we want to help you avoid your stomach feeling like it's falling through the floor when you present to your leadership team. We want to help you avoid even being asked that uncomfortable 'So what?' question.

By now you know the many advantages of using storylines. They help you refine your thinking and communicate with confidence and clarity, they save time, and they lead to quicker and better decisions, all of which add up to improved business performance. We have provided you with a way of thinking through your ideas so you can organise them logically, whether working from scratch or using one of our patterns. We have also shown you how to convert your storyline into a piece of Word or PowerPoint communication.

But, where should you start? Here are some ideas to help you get going:

- **Start with small, routine pieces of communication** so that the effort required to make improvements is small. Emails are the best place to start. We suggest committing to consciously applying storylining principles to three emails per day for the first week so you can build some momentum. Increase the number or proportion of emails you will consciously apply the ideas to in subsequent weeks. Hand-written notes for presenting your ideas in meetings are also a practical, low-risk thing to try, and are great for building your skills.

- **Involve a colleague for more complex pieces of communication.** If they haven't read this book, you could explain briefly what you are aiming to do and then offer them the 10-point test as a guide to think through their feedback for you. Although they are unlikely to be able to explain why your top line supporting points do or don't belong together, they will certainly be able to help you with your introduction, answer, audience needs, and whether the storyline is MECE or not.

  If you are starting to feel confident with your storylining ability, you may also like to take one or more team members to a whiteboard and think through a storyline together. We find this to be hugely productive, particularly when people reciprocate with their support. Don't underestimate the value of fresh eyes on storylines. An objective outsider can push your logic, and collaborating to think through ideas helps teams keep across each other's activities too.

- **Explain to high-stakes audiences that you are trying something new** before sending them a new document, which might look quite different to previous ones. Hopefully the positive response from your emails will give you courage to try on riskier pieces of communication, but even so some audiences benefit from forewarning, particularly where templates are currently being used. We have often found that they enjoy being asked for their reaction to the new approach. They like to know you are taking your role seriously and are striving for improvements, and they also like to be asked.

- **Stick with it!** It is very easy to gain a small amount of benefit from a new idea and then move quickly onto the next shiny new thing. We expect you will see a positive difference in the responses you get quite quickly, but being good at storylining is a bit like being fit: if you stop exercising, you stop being fit.

We hope this book has helped you, and wish you all the very best with improving your ability to answer – and ideally avoid altogether – that 'So what?' question.

Davina and Gerard

APPENDIX A

A STORYLINE DEVELOPED INTO A WORD DOCUMENT

Building a storyline is on its own a very useful thing to do, but more often than not a storyline needs to be converted into a Word or Power-Point (or similar) document. To help you understand this conversion process, here's an example storyline and the correlated Word document. Have a look at the storyline, and then read the Word document to see how the elements from the storyline are incorporated into the document.

We hope you find this useful. (This expands on the Coonawarra Corp example from chapters 1 and 3.)

Coonawarra Corp should invest in Black's intelligent cloud-based storage solution

Context	As you will recall from recent conversations, effective cloud-based data management is increasingly critical to Coonawarra Corp's technology strategy
Trigger	We've undertaken a review to help us decide how to manage key elements of one component: intelligent cloud-based data storage capabilities
Question	How should we manage intelligent cloud-based data storage?

Coonawarra Corp should invest $300K–$400K in Black to ensure it has intelligent cloud-based data storage capabilities

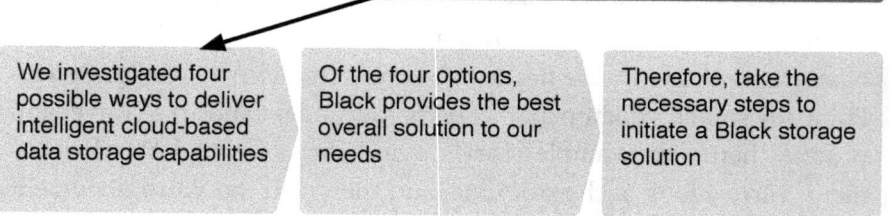

We investigated four possible ways to deliver intelligent cloud-based data storage capabilities	Of the four options, Black provides the best overall solution to our needs	Therefore, take the necessary steps to initiate a Black storage solution
A We investigated outsourcing to Yellow as competitor A has done so B We investigated working with Black given our historic relationship C We considered Pink given competitor B has used Pink's technology successfully D We considered insourcing given the IT team is excited by the challenge and it would broaden their capabilities	• Black meets all key requirements • Yellow meets many of the basic requirements but lacks industry maturity • Pink could meet the basic requirements as a retrofit to current storage but adoption of their technology introduces unneeded complexity • Managing it internally is not possible as we lack the skills	• Allocate $300K–$400K • Agree partnering arrangements with Black • Develop a data migration plan • Develop a risk management plan

Invest $300K to $400K in Black Inc. to build Intelligent Cloud-Based Data Storage

As you will recall from our recent conversations, effective cloud-based data management is increasingly critical to Coonawarra Corp's technology strategy. We have undertaken a review to help us decide how to deliver intelligent cloud-based data storage capabilities – looking at internal and external opportunities.

We recommend that Coonawarra Corp invest $300K to $400K in the Black Inc. solution to ensure Coonawarra has intelligent cloud-based data storage capabilities. Our key findings are outlined below.

- We investigated four options to deliver intelligent cloud-based data storage capabilities.

- Of the four options, we think Black Inc. provides the best solution for our needs.

- As a result, we recommend undertaking a 10-week program to initiate the migration to Black.

Below, I discuss each of the above points in more detail.

Four options to deliver intelligent cloud-based data storage capabilities

There are four potential options to deliver intelligent cloud-based data storage capabilities. They are:

1. Outsourcing to Yellow Company: three similar organisations have recently outsourced their data storage needs to Yellow.

2. Outsourcing to Black Inc. who have a well-known cloud solution and who also currently provide three of our major IT systems.

3. Purchasing tools and technology from Pink Corporation: another similar organistion successfully implemented Pink Corporation's technology for data storage.

4. Insourcing to our IT team: our IT team could potentially design and deliver a cloud strategy with sufficient resources and a capability build.

Of the four, Black Inc. provides the best solution for our needs

We evaluated these four options against five criteria: the quality of the cloud technology solution, cost, industry maturity of the provider, complexity of the implementation solution, and the provider's ability to execute. Overall, we recommend outsourcing to Black Inc. because they score highest against the key criteria. Exhibit 1 shows our summary analysis.

Black provides the best overall storage solution

Options	Technology	Cost	Maturity	Complexity	Resources	Comments
Use internal resources	✓	✗	✓	✗	✗	• Possible but will be more than $500K cost and lack of specialist skills
Black	✓	✓	✓	✓	✓	• Good technology • Known quantity – worked with us before • In budget $300K-400K
Yellow	✓	✓	✗	?	?	• Good technology • Very new start up – resources and ability to execute unclear
Pink	✓	?	✓	✗	?	• Solid technology but requires retrofit • Introduces complexity in implementation and possible cost

Here is how each of the options stacks up.

Option 1 – Outsourcing to Yellow Company is possible but risky

The option to outsource to Yellow Company scores well on technology and cost, but is risky. This option would:

1. Allow us to leverage Yellow's technology which is rated strongly in the industry.

2. Achieve a cost-effective solution because outsourcing to Yellow has the second lowest overall price among the four options considered.

3. Expose us to risks due to their questionable scores on maturity, complexity and resources. Since Yellow is a new start-up, the maturity of their team, resources and ability to execute are unclear.

Option 2 – Purchasing tools and technology from Pink Corporation is overly complicated

The option to purchase tools and technology from Pink Corporation scores very well on technology and maturity as Pink have a long track record. However, this option would:

1. Require retrofitting Pink's technology, resulting in higher costs that exceed the budget.

2. Present implementation risk because Pink is limited on resources for this scale of project.

Option 3 – Insourcing to our internal IT team is possible, but expensive and risky

Our internal IT team could potentially build this capability and it would provide control over the build. However, this option presents the following downsides:

1. Our IT team lacks the resources and advanced skills necessary to manage this level of integration complexity.

2. Their cost estimate is more than $500,000–$1,000,000, which exceeds the budget.

Option 4 – Outsourcing to Black Inc. meets all criteria

Our analysis showed that outsourcing to Black Inc. is the most attractive option:

1. They have an excellent technical solution as recognised by Gartner Inc.

2. We have confidence in their resources and ability to handle a complex implementation since they have worked with us in the past and have delivered similar builds for similar organsations of our scale and complexity.

3. Their solution is cost-competitive and within our target budget of less than $500k.

Recommend initiate the migration to Black

Given the evaluation above, we recommend Coonawarra initiates a 10-week program to migrate to a cloud-based data storage solution with Black Inc. There are four key actions we need to take to move this forward:

1. Ask the executive leadership team to approve this plan and allocate $300K–$400K at our staff meeting next week.

2. Develop a data migration plan. I estimate this will take about four weeks to complete.

3. Develop a risk management plan. I estimate this will take about three weeks to complete.

4. Go live with the implementation. This would take about six weeks to implement.

* * *

Please let me know if you have any additional questions or concerns.

Source: Phil, a participant from Davina's Clarity First Online Group Coaching Program who converted the storyline into the paper as a learning exercise.

APPENDIX B

A STORYLINE DEVELOPED INTO A POWERPOINT PACK

In the spirit of making storylines useful and practical, here's an example of a storyline being fleshed out as a PowerPoint pack. To illustrate this fully we have included a storyline, a storyboard mapping that storyline into the shape of a pack, and then the pages within the pack.

For the sake of simplicity we have used a storyline referenced earlier in the book (in chapter 3).

Coonawarra Corp should invest in Black's intelligent cloud-based storage solution

Context	As you will recall from recent conversations, effective cloud-based data management is increasingly critical to Coonawarra Corp's technology strategy
Trigger	We've undertaken a review to help us decide how to manage key elements of one component: intelligent cloud-based data storage capabilities
Question	How should we manage intelligent cloud-based data storage?

Coonawarra Corp should invest $300K–$400K in Black to ensure it has intelligent cloud-based data storage capabilities

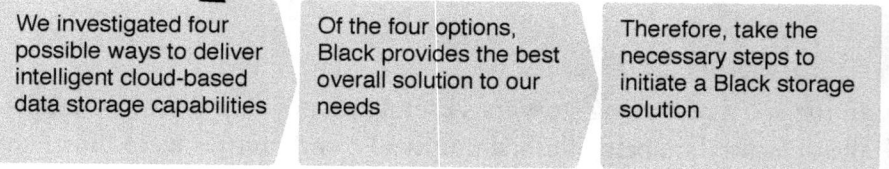

We investigated four possible ways to deliver intelligent cloud-based data storage capabilities	Of the four options, Black provides the best overall solution to our needs	Therefore, take the necessary steps to initiate a Black storage solution
A We investigated outsourcing to Yellow as competitor A has done so	• Black meets all key requirements	• Allocate $300K–$400K
B We investigated working with Black given our historic relationship	• Yellow meets many of the basic requirements but lacks industry maturity	• Agree partnering arrangements with Black
C We considered Pink given competitor B has used Pink's technology successfully	• Pink could meet the basic requirements as a retrofit to current storage but adoption of their technology introduces unneeded complexity	• Develop a data migration plan • Develop a risk management plan
D We considered insourcing given the IT team is excited by the challenge and it would broaden their capabilities	• Managing it internally is not possible as we lack the skills	

This pack tells the story

- Provides title, date and description of pack

- Explains purpose and background of pack
- Avoids controversy
- Describes structure: sections, appendices, etc.

- Works like an executive summary
- States So what
- Provides overview of storyline
- Use a visual if appropriate

- Tracker can be used to show audience where you are in the story

Building intelligent cloud-based data storage capabilities

Discussion pack | September 2018

Background

As you will recall from recent conversations, effective cloud based data management is increasingly critical to Coonawarra Corp's technology strategy

We've undertaken a review to help us decide how to manage key elements of one component: intelligent cloud-based data storage capabilities

This deck summarises our findings about what actions Coonawarra should take.

Susan
IT Manager
September 2018

Clarity

Coonawarra Corp should invest $300K-$400K in Black **to ensure it has intelligent cloud-based data storage capabilities**

We investigated four possible ways to deliver intelligent cloud-based data storage capabilities

Black provides the best overall solution to our needs

Therefore take the necessary steps to initiate a Black storage solution

Clarity

We investigated four possible ways **to deliver intelligent cloud-based data storage capabilities**

Options	Description
A. Outsourcing completely to Yellow	• Competitor A has recently outsourced to Yellow
B. Partnering with Black	• We have a strong existing relationship through previous projects
C. Purchasing tools and technology from Pink	• Competitor B incorporated Pink's technology successfully
D. Managing the issue internally	• The IT team is excited by this challenge as it would enable them to broaden out their own capabilities

Clarity

Black provides the best overall storage solution

Options	Technology	Cost	Maturity	Complexity	Resources	Comments
Use internal resources	✓	✕	✓	✕	✕	• Possible but will be more than $500K cost and lack of specialist skills
Black	✓	✓	✓	✓	✓	• Good technology • Known quantity – worked with us before • In budget $300K-400K
Yellow	✓	✓	✕	?	?	• Good technology • Very new start up – resources and ability to execute unclear
Pink	✓	?	✓	✕	?	• Solid technology but requires retrofit • Introduces complexity in implementation and possible cost

Clarity

We recommend that Coonawarra take necessary steps to initiate a Black storage solution

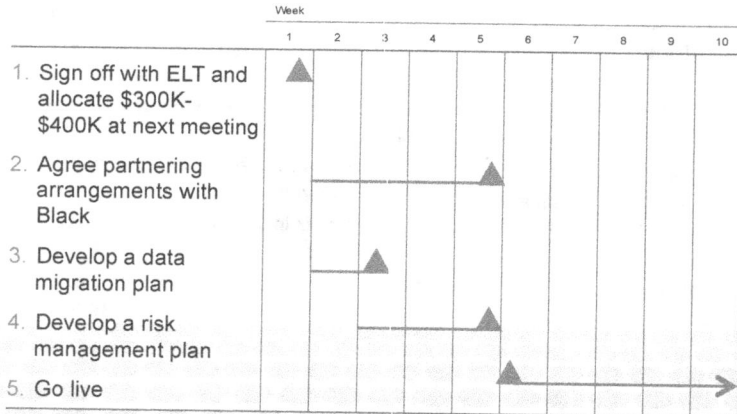

	Week 1	2	3	4	5	6	7	8	9	10
1. Sign off with ELT and allocate $300K-$400K at next meeting										
2. Agree partnering arrangements with Black										
3. Develop a data migration plan										
4. Develop a risk management plan										
5. Go live										

Clarity

126

ABOUT DAVINA
AND GERARD

Davina Stanley and Gerard Castles have been helping professionals use storylines for decades. Trained at McKinsey & Company in Hong Kong and in Sydney, the two spread their wings to work independently before starting Clarity Thought Partners together in 2010.

Davina is Managing Director of Clarity Thought Partners. Davina blends her education and consulting experience to design and deliver innovative and engaging programs for clients. Having begun her working life as a school teacher, she retrained and moved into corporate affairs in a multinational company before joining McKinsey in Hong Kong as a communication specialist. She worked for The Firm in a range of full-time, part-time and freelance capacities over 18 years, helping consultants clarify their thinking so they could communicate clearly with their clients. She now supports the partners and consultants from another top-tier firm, as well as many other clients.

Gerard is Co-Founder of Clarity Thought Partners. Gerard blends his straight-talking abilities with a sharp intellect and a great sense of humour to help his clients get to the point quickly. Having also begun his career as a school teacher, Gerard joined McKinsey in Sydney in 1987, where he was one of the most respected communication specialists globally. He branched out on his own seven years later to help clients with their communication and change management projects, where he has won awards for the quality of his work. Gerard is about as connected as you can get in Australian business. He has worked with people at every level of business, consulting and government, and is at times referred to in the press as a 'nameless consultant' helping 'so and so'. McKinsey still calls Gerard to help on discrete client projects.

RESOURCES

Here are some tools you may find useful.

Our website (http://claritycollege.co) offers free tools to help you build your storylines:

- Blank PowerPoint templates that you can use to prepare your storylines (see the free stuff under 'courses').

- The 'Big Idea' newsletter, which offers occasional case studies and insights designed to help you master storylining in your own work (also in the free stuff section).

- Short articles, including three tips to help technical experts communicate clearly. One example is *The Tale of Two Stories*, a short article and a video describing the decision-making process required to communicate with both the board and the leadership team about the same issue. Find it at http://claritycollege.co/engaging-multiple-audiences-the-tale-of-two-stories/

Our courses teach you how to build storylines so you can have greater influence online:

- **Clarity Concepts:** this 10-module online course introduces the concepts we have discussed in detail, provides challenges to help you test your understanding and put the ideas into practice, as well as a handout for each module and access to in-depth FAQs.

- **Clarity First Online Group Coaching Program:** this interactive three-month university-style course enables you to learn and master storylining techniques across a wide range of situations. Go to http://clarityfirstprogram.com to learn more.

BIBLIOGRAPHY

Bolton, Robert & Grover-Bolton, Dorothy, 1996, *People Styles at Work: Making bad relationships good and good relationships better*, American Management Association.

Butcher, S H, 1997, Aristotle, *Poetics*, Dover Thrift Editions.

Carrick, Nancy & Finsen, Lawrence, 1997, *The Persuasive Pen: An integrated approach to reasoning and writing*, Jones and Bartlett Publishers.

Friga, Paul N, 2008, *The McKinsey Engagement: A powerful toolkit for more efficient and effective team problem solving*, McGraw-Hill.

Kolko, Jon, 2010, *Design Issues*, 'Abductive Thinking and Sensemaking: The Drivers of Design Synthesis', Volume 26, Number 1.

Long, Linda, 2002, *The Power of Logic in Problem Solving and Communication*, self-published.

McKinsey & Company, *The McKinsey Quarterly*, 'The Psychology of Change Management', 2003 Special Edition.

Minto, Barbara, 2010, *The Minto Pyramid Principle: Logic in writing, thinking and problem solving*, self-published.

Rasiel, Ethan M & Friga Paul N, 2002, *The McKinsey Mind*, McGraw-Hill.

Shaw, Patrick, 1997, *Logic and its Limits*, 2nd edn, Oxford University Press.

Talbot, Marianne, 'Lessons in Logic', https://mariannetalbot.co.uk.

Thompson, Peter, 1998, *Persuading Aristotle*, Allen & Unwin.

Van Gelder, Tim, Discussions on MECE and similar topics at https://timvangelder.com.

Watanabe, Ken, 2009, *Problem Solving 101*, Random House.

Zelazny, Gene, 2001, *Say it with Charts: The executive's guide to visual communication*, 4th edn, McGraw-Hill.

Zelazny, Gene, 2006, *Say it with Presentations: How to design and deliver successful business presentations*, 2nd edn, McGraw-Hill.

CLARITY FIRST
GROUP
COACHING
P R O G R A M

For technical experts who want to get out of the details so they can communicate with greater impact

www.clarityfirstprogram.com